HOW TO DRAW
VEHICLES

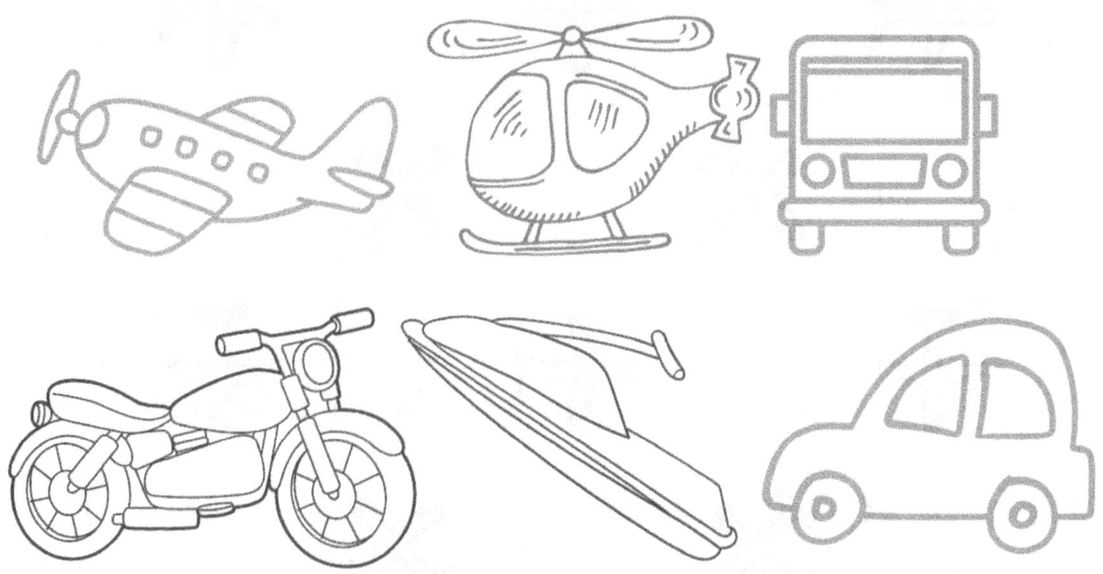

This Book Belongs To

....

By Rowan Forest

About The Author

Rowan Forest is a passionate author from Australia, specializing in creating engaging books for both children and adults. With a background in Information Technology, Rowan's love for design and creativity was sparked while nurturing his children's artistic talents. His natural design skills and gift for captivating young readers are reflected in his books, which are filled with exciting adventures and puzzles that inspire imagination and creativity.

Rowan's how-to-draw books provide simple instructions that make drawing accessible and enjoyable for readers of all ages. His coloring books offer a vibrant and interactive way for them to express their creativity, while his word search puzzles are designed to challenge and improve their cognitive skills and vocabulary.

With an unwavering commitment to excellence, Rowan is always experimenting with new ideas and writing styles to entertain and engage his readers.

CAR
SCOOTER
AIRPLANE
AIR BALLON
BOAT
ROCKET
BUS
TRUCK
CYCLE
SUBMARINE
SHIP
BIKE
HELICOPTER
& MORE

How To Use This Book

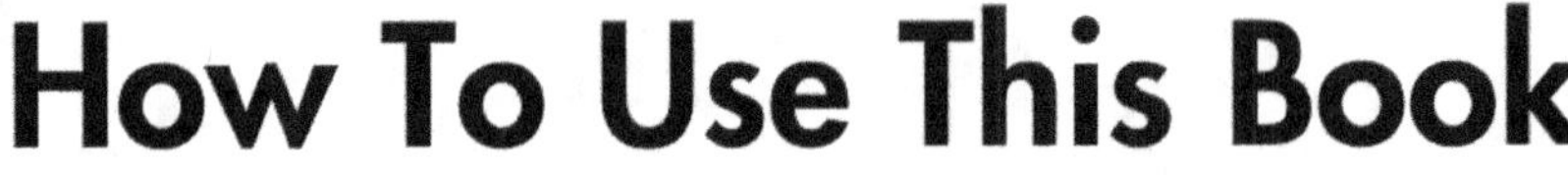

- Get a sharp pencil and an eraser ready

- Draw the black lines from the first drawing

- Add the black lines from each additional step

- If you get stuck, look at the final drawing

- After completing the drawing, you can color it in any way you like

Start by drawing lightly so that any mistakes can be easily erased

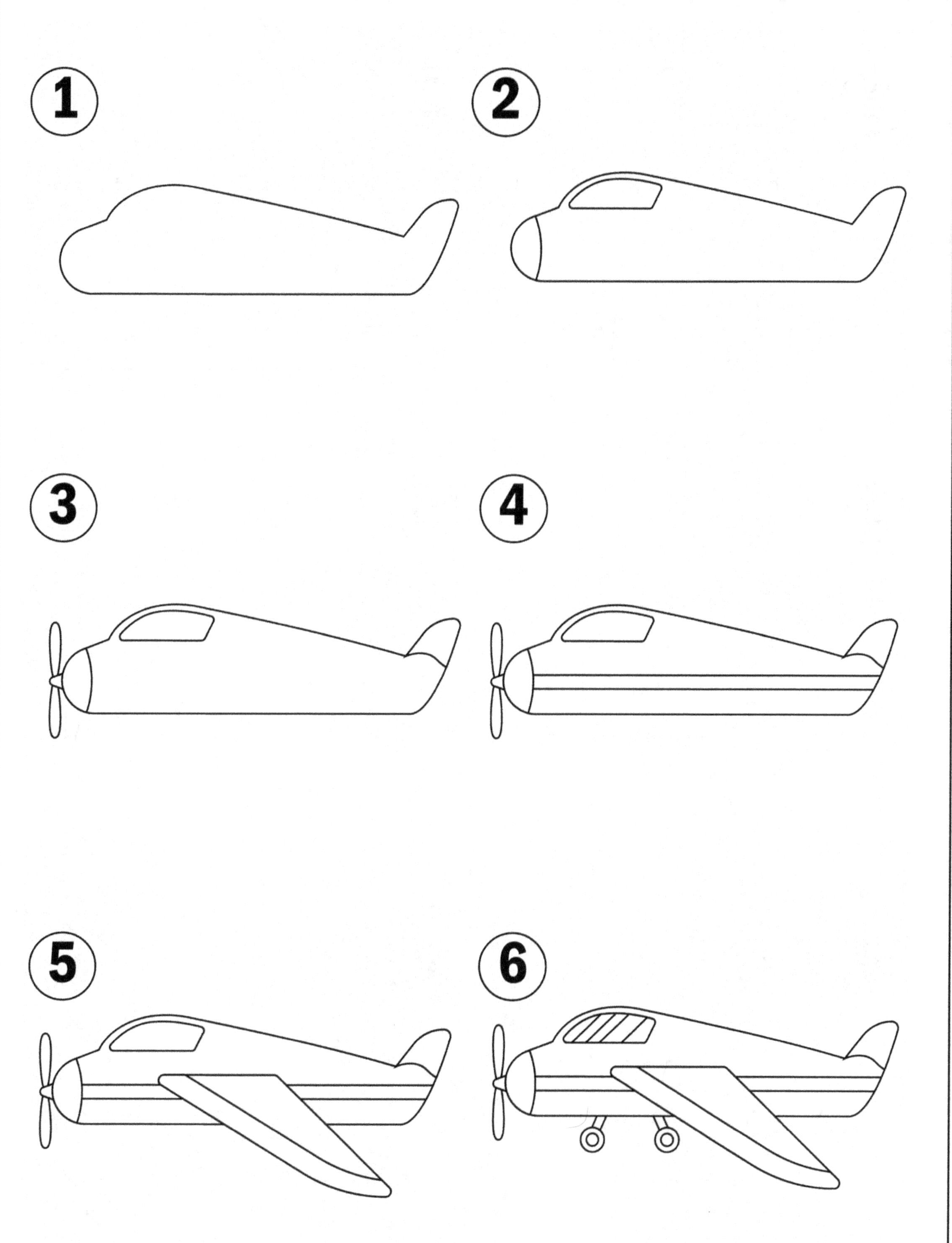

1
2
3
4
5
6

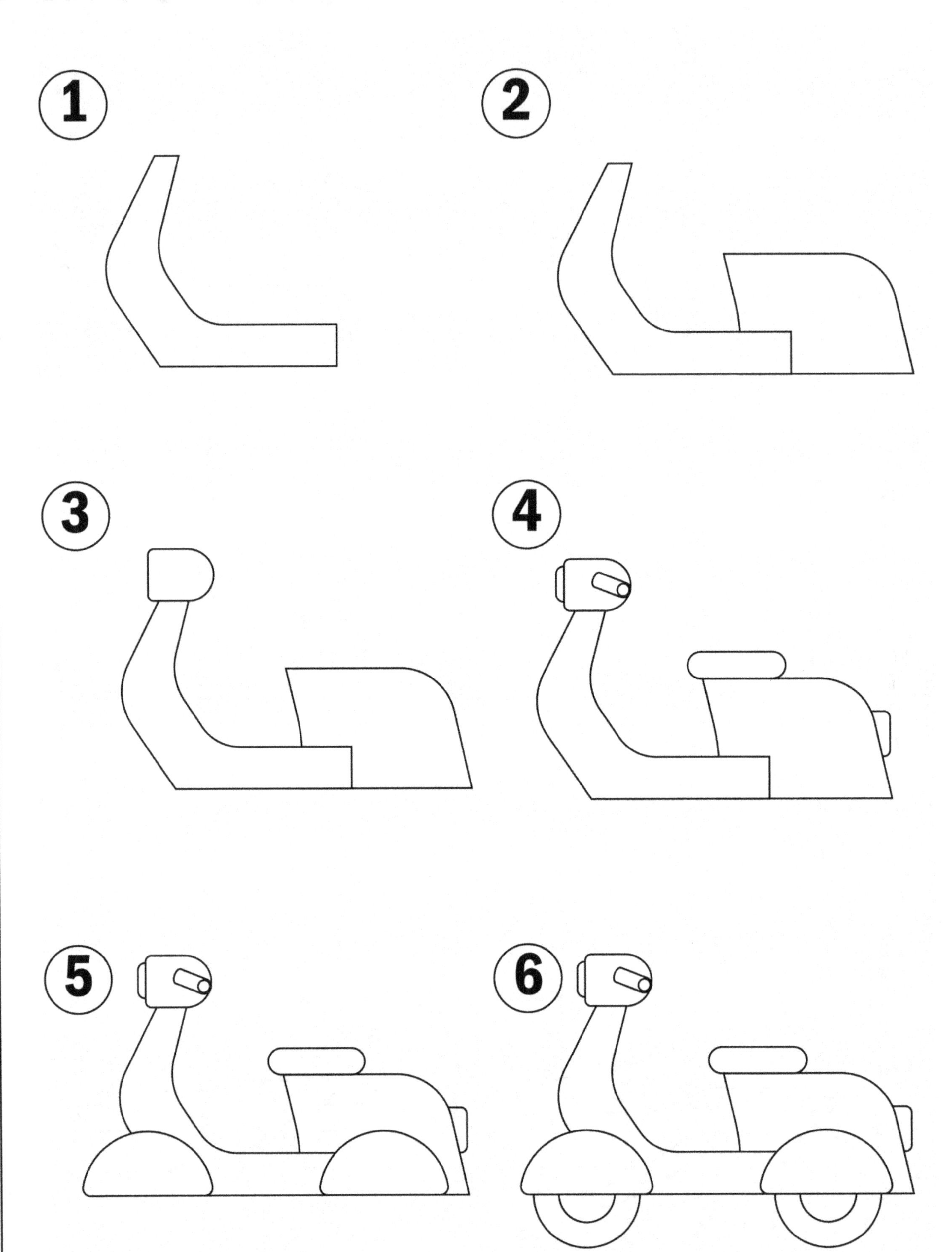

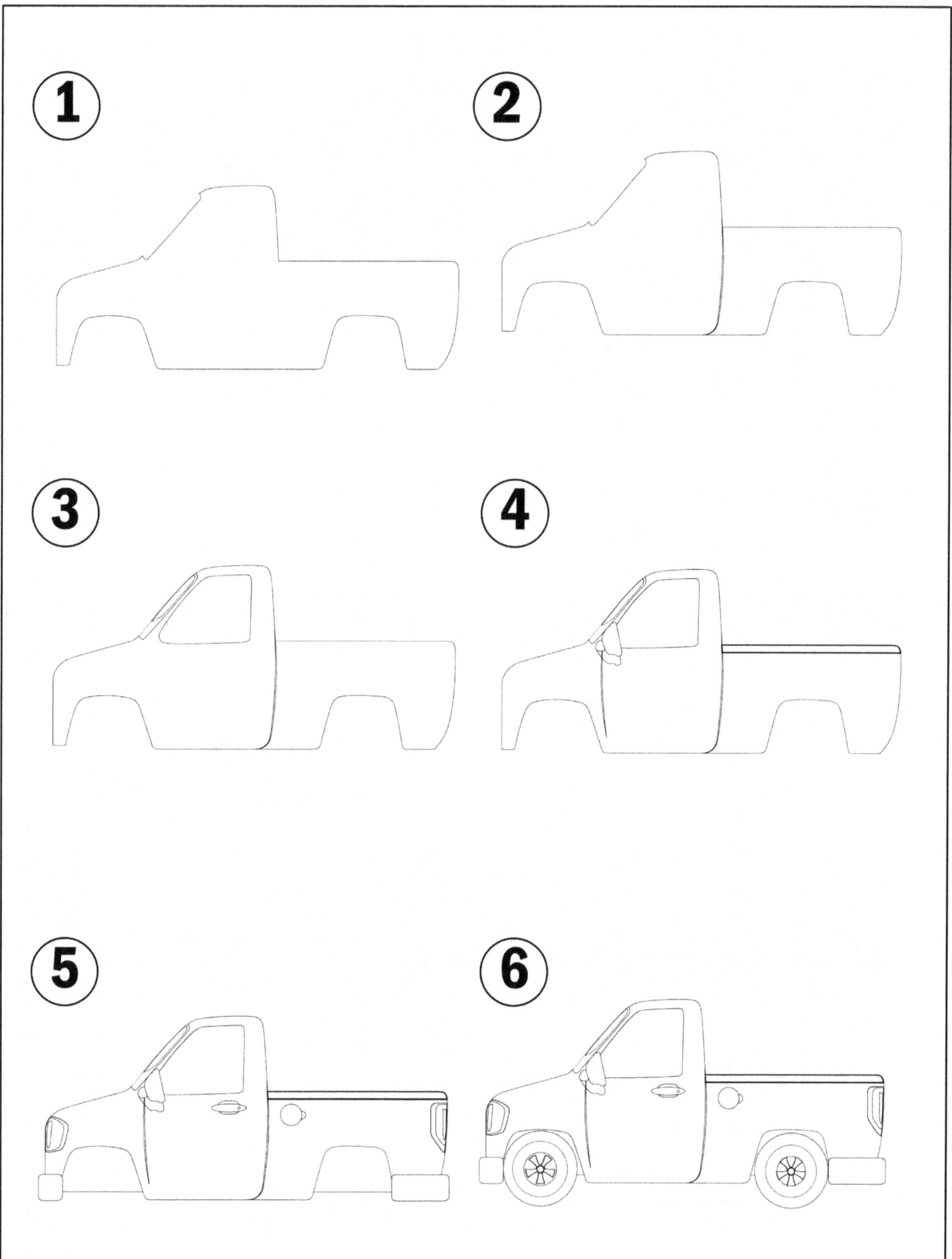

1
2
3
4
5
6

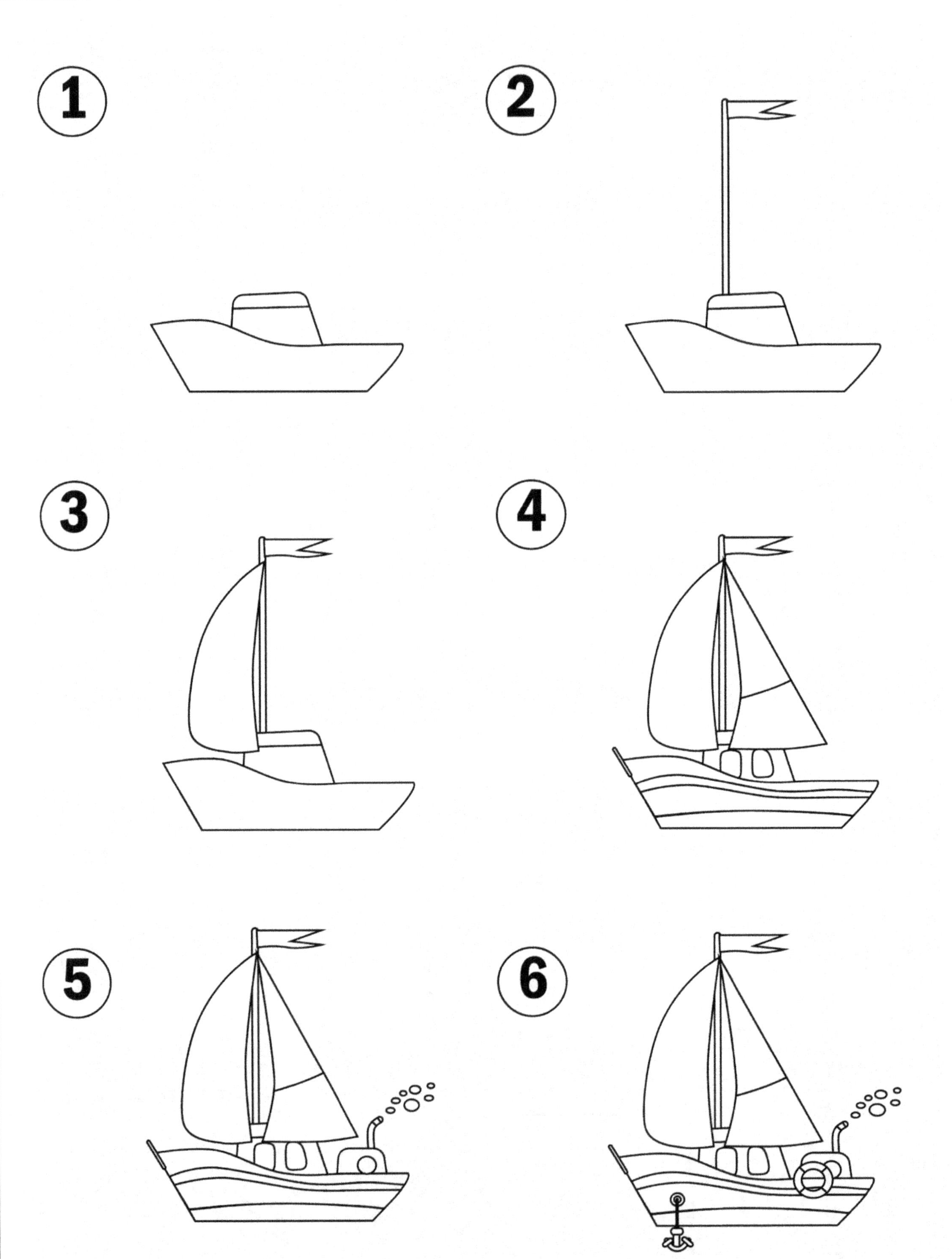

1
2
3
4
5
6

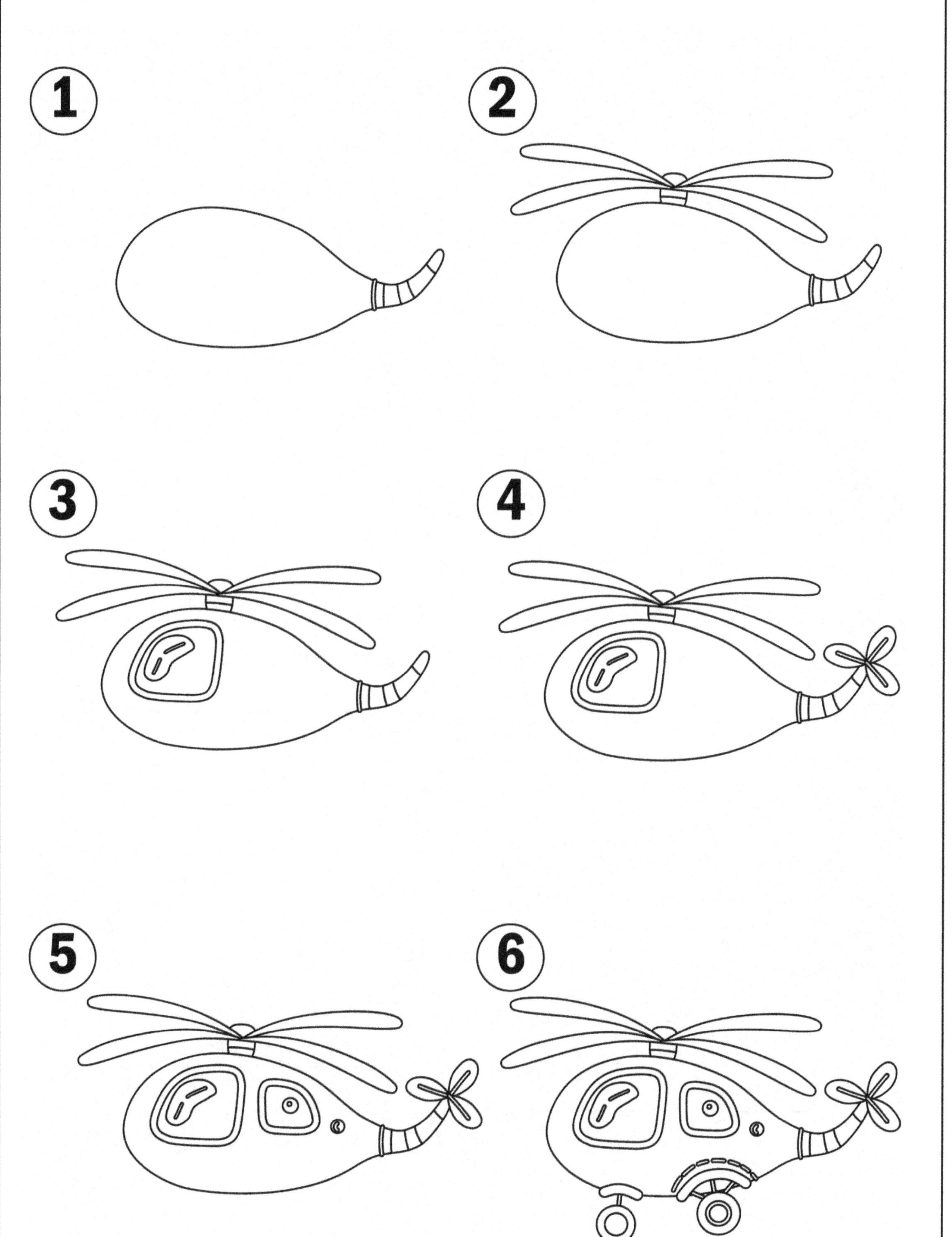

1
2
3
4
5
6

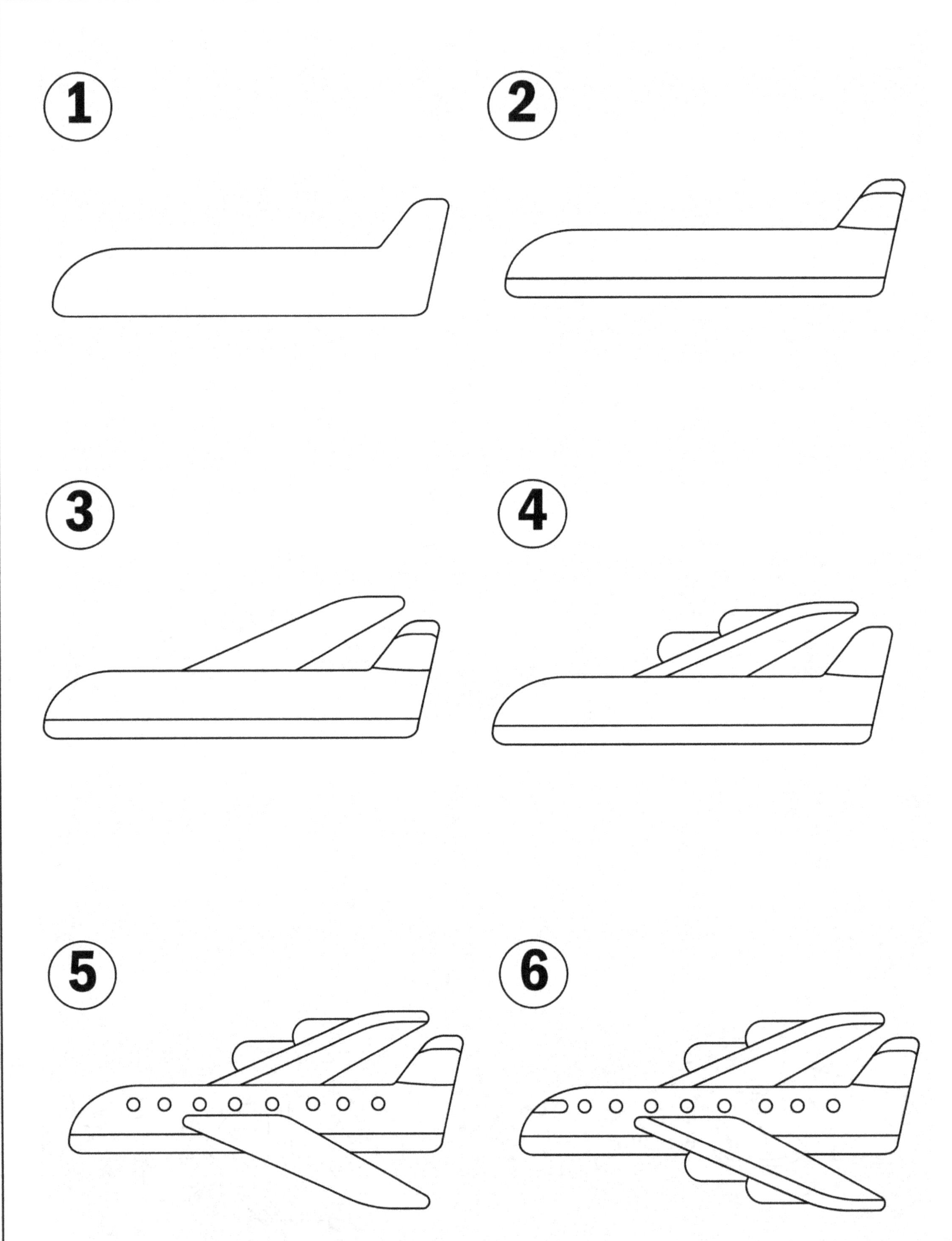

1
2
3
4
5
6

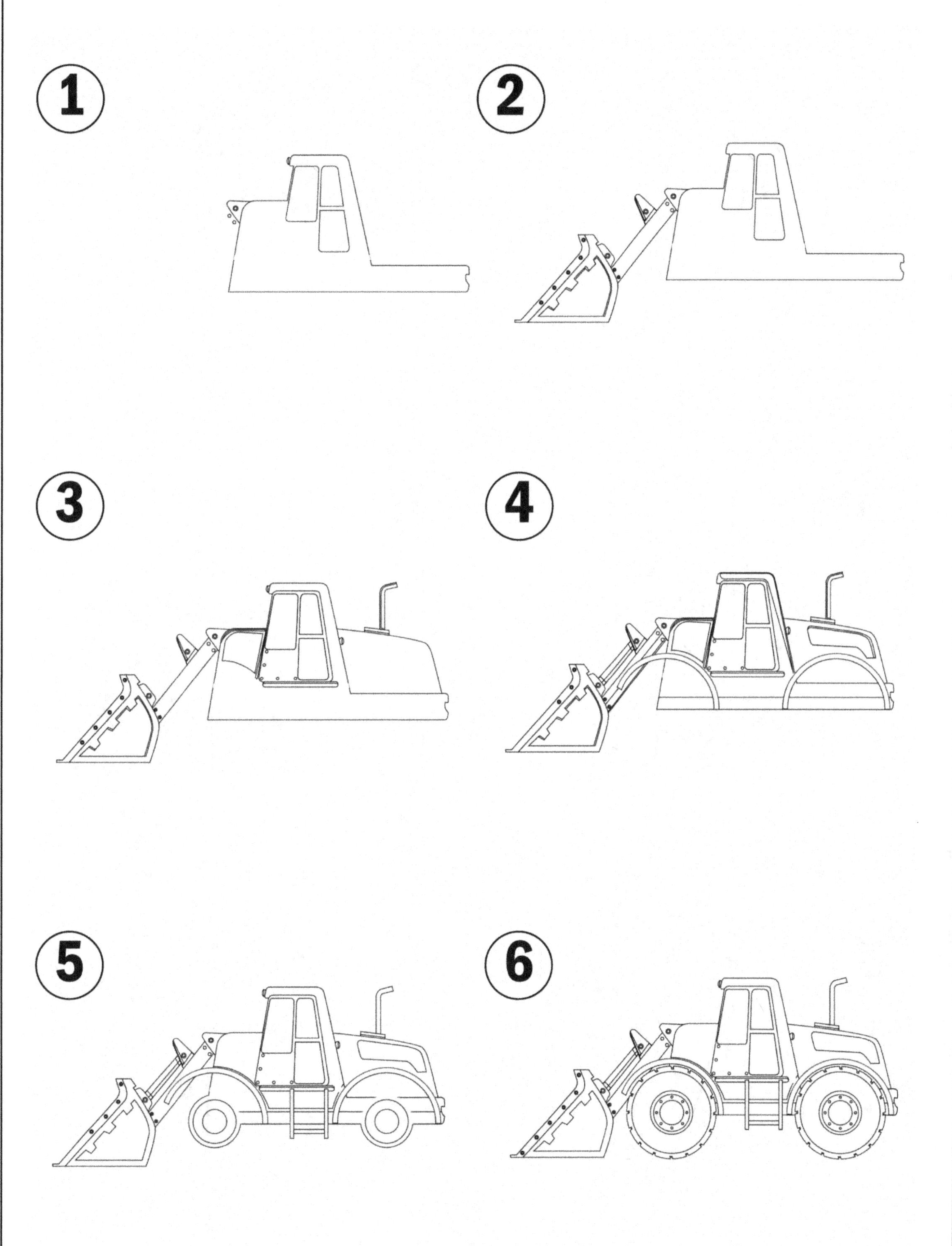

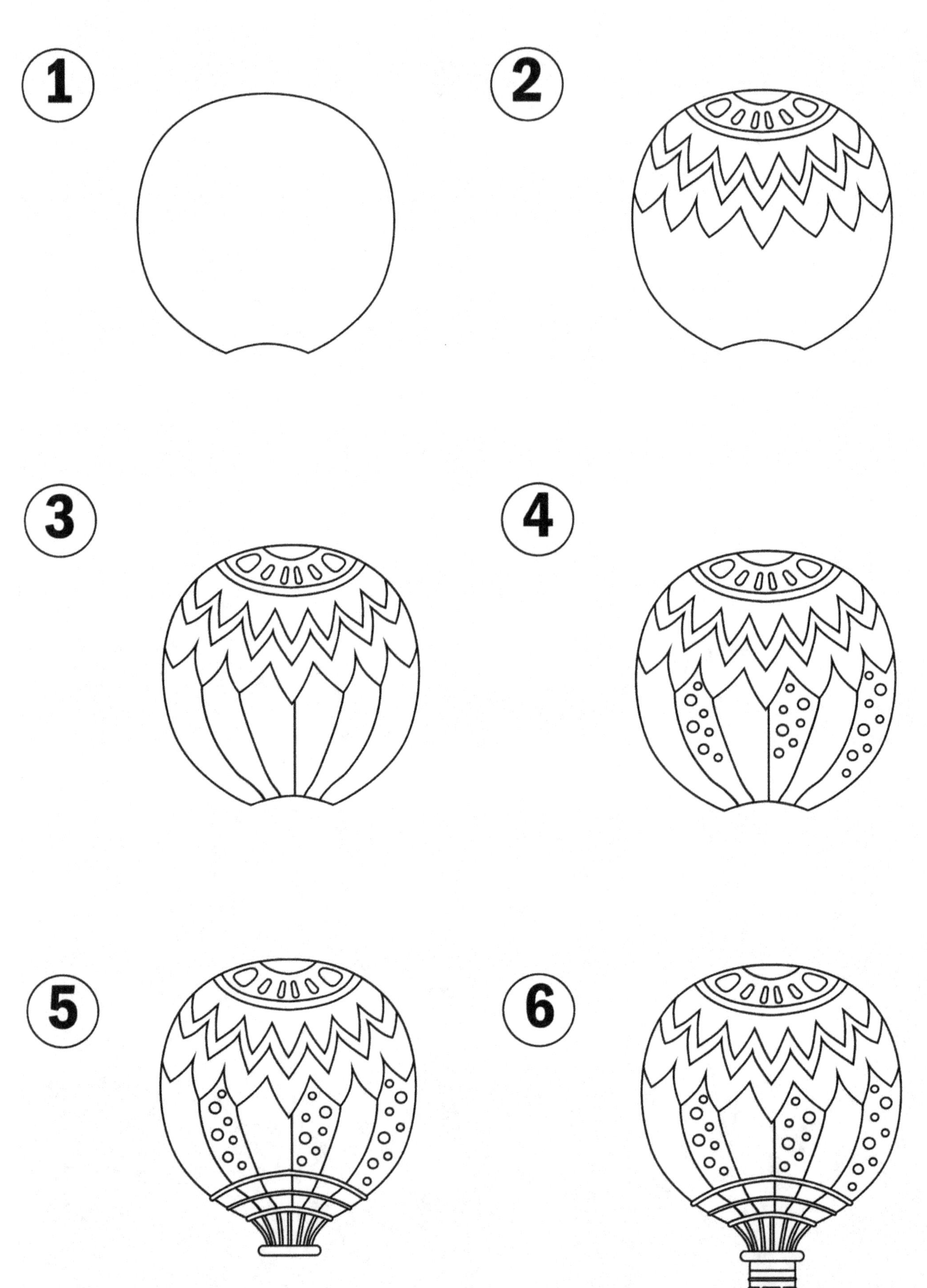

1
2
3
4
5
6

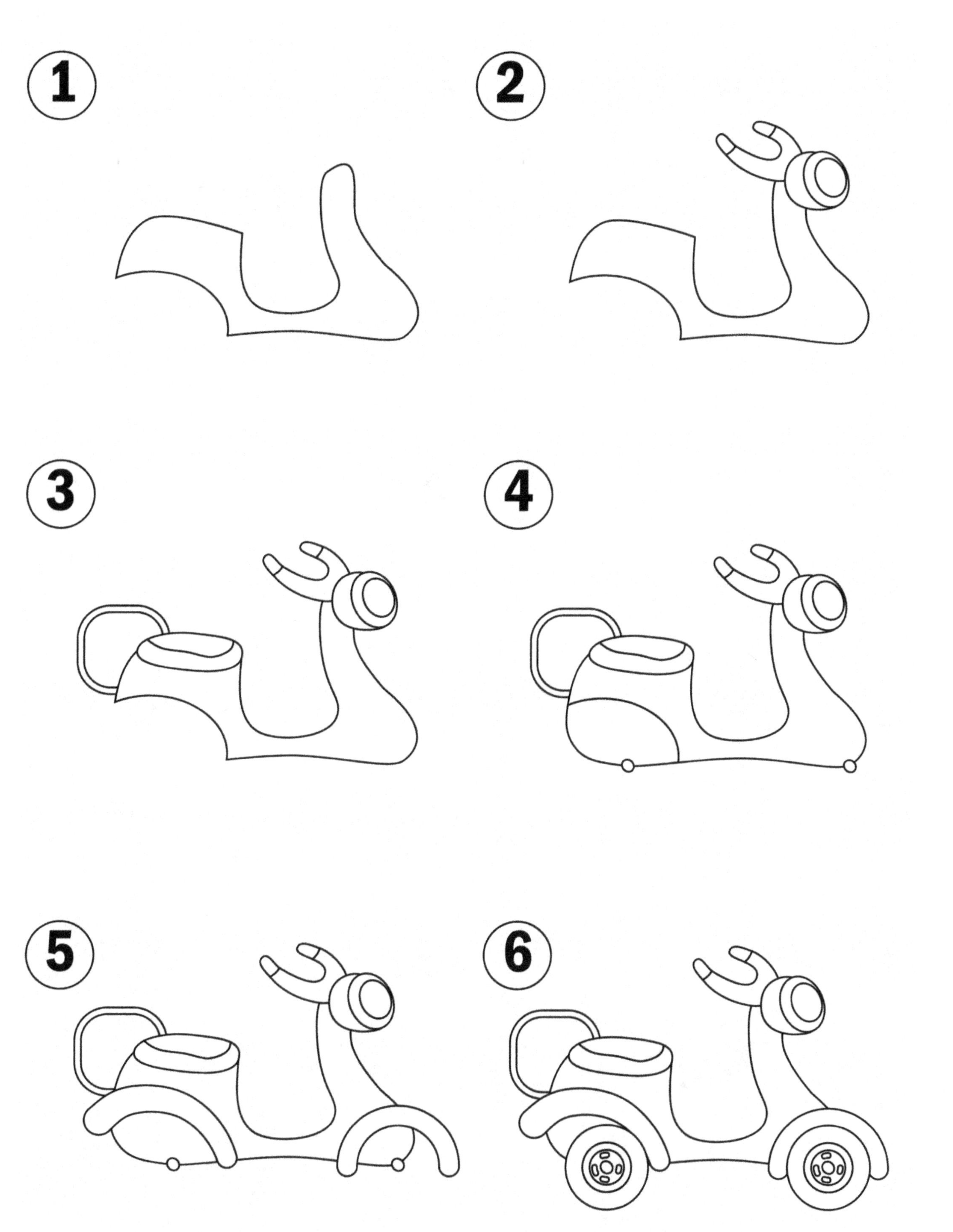

1
2
3
4
5
6

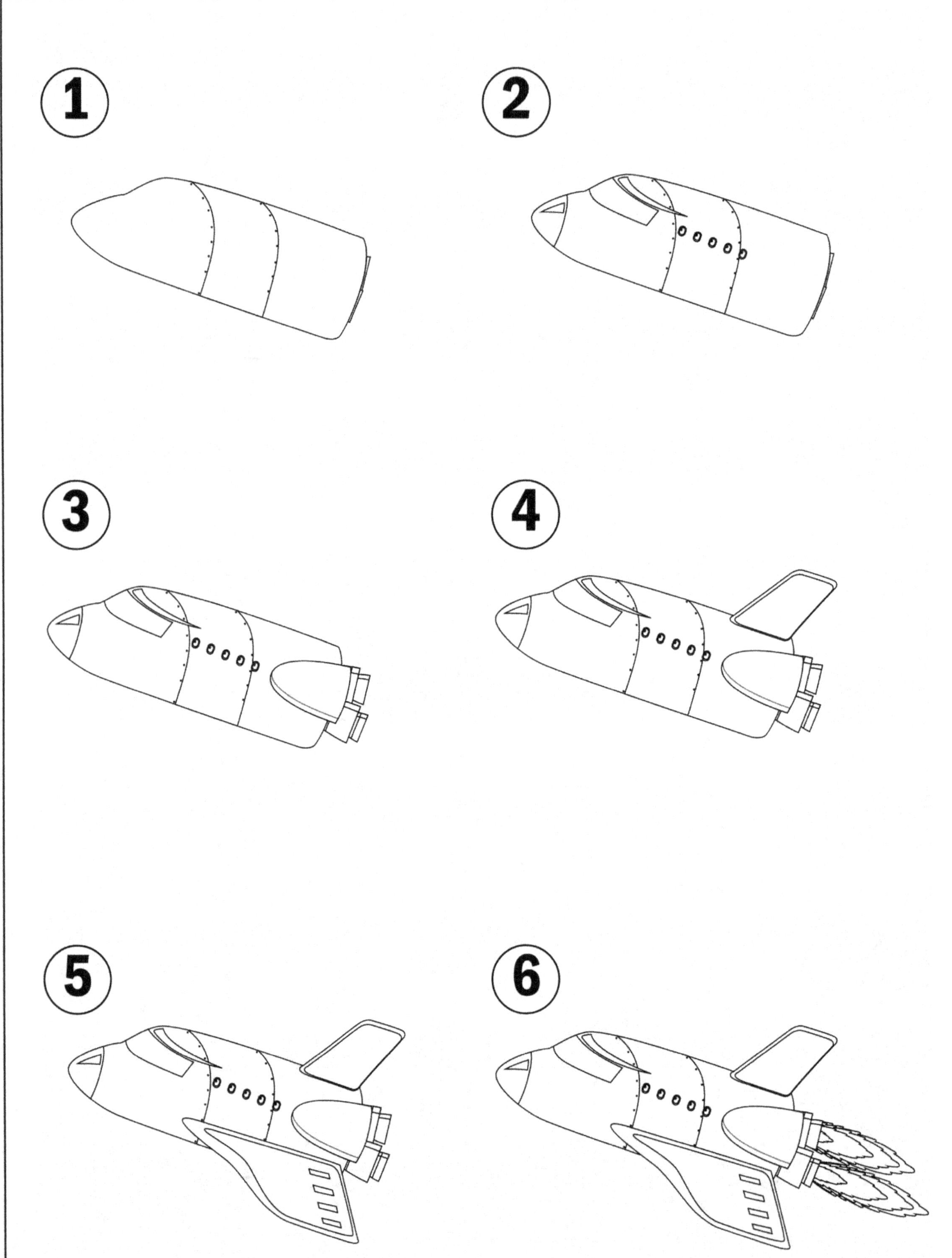

1
2
3
4
5
6

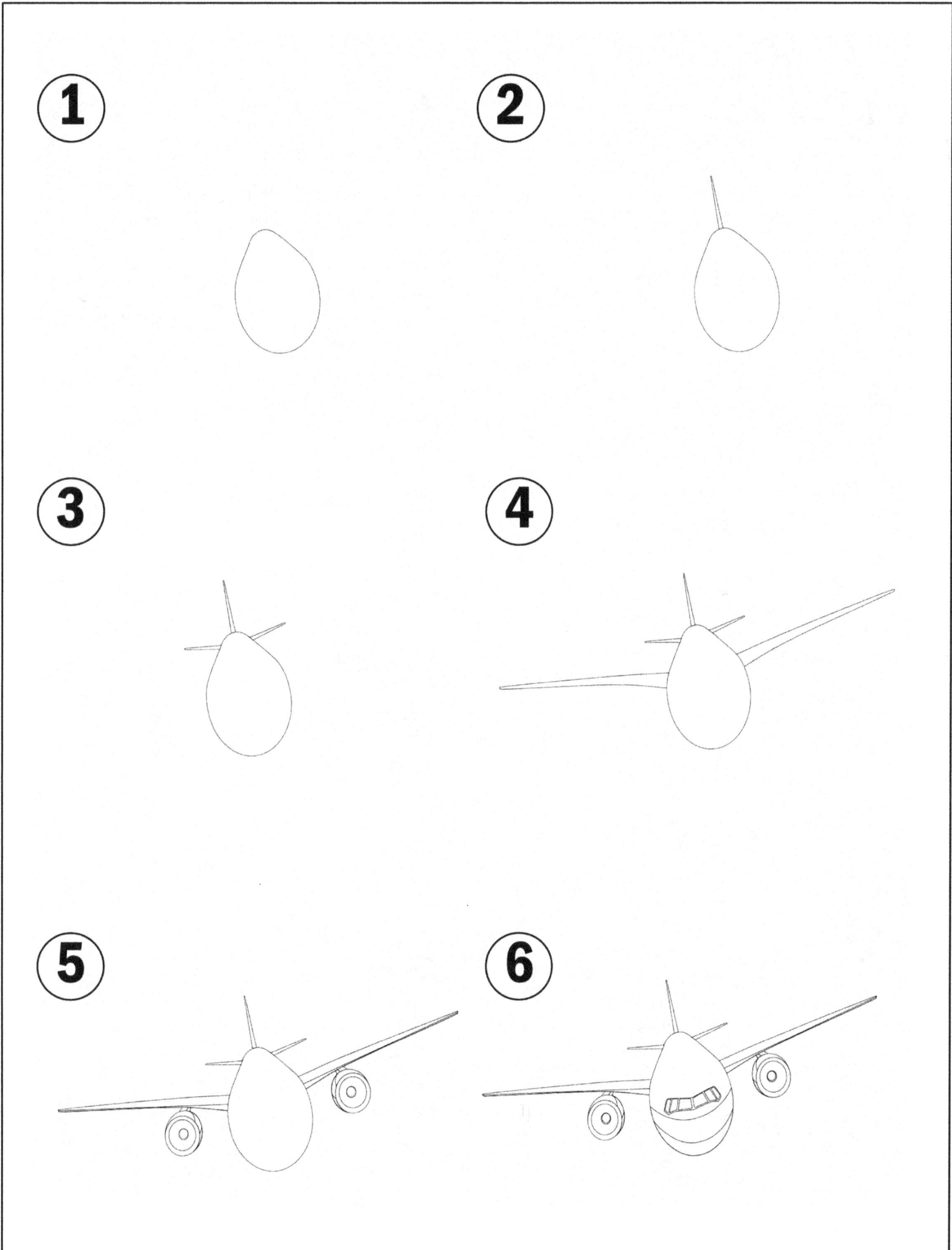

1
2
3
4
5
6

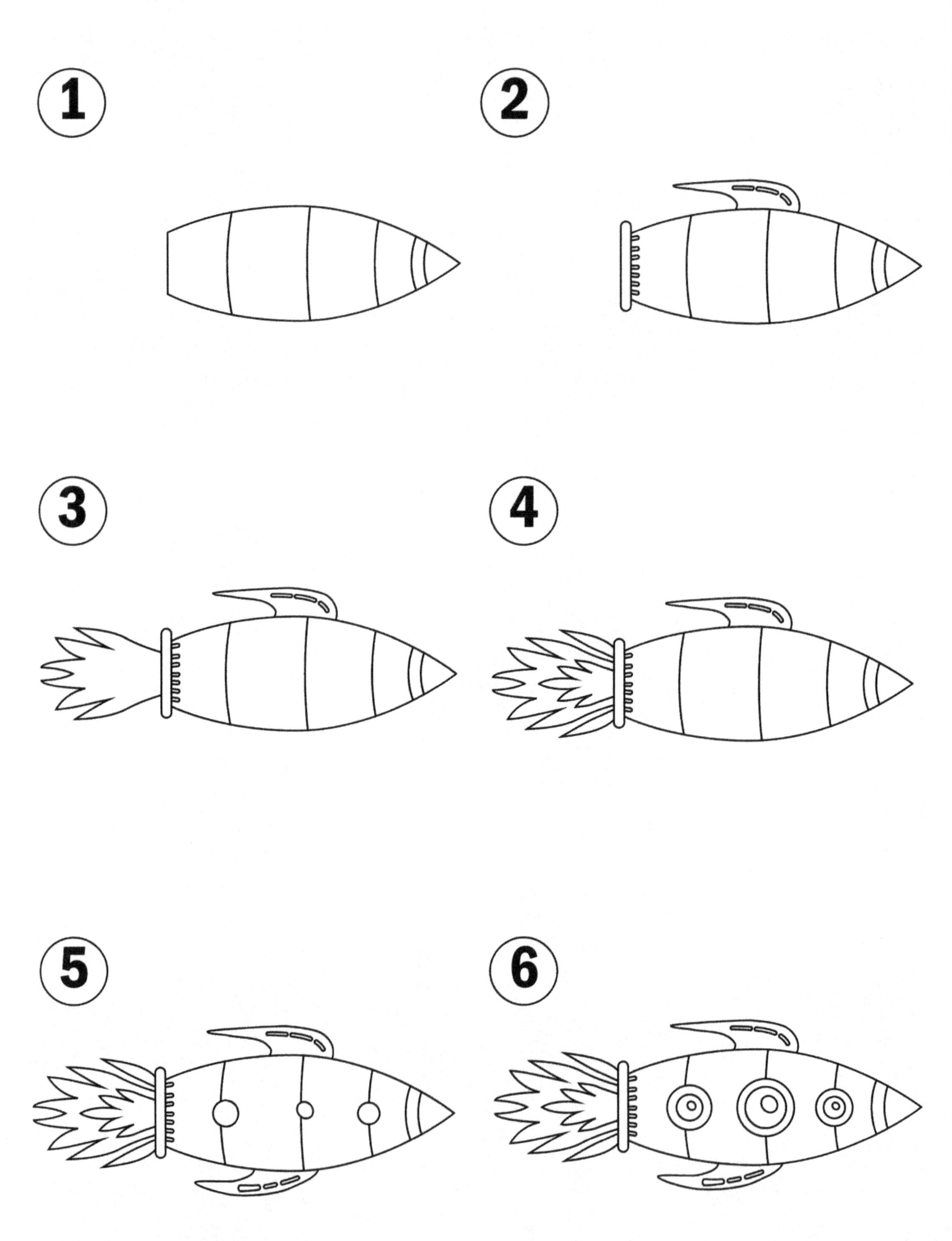

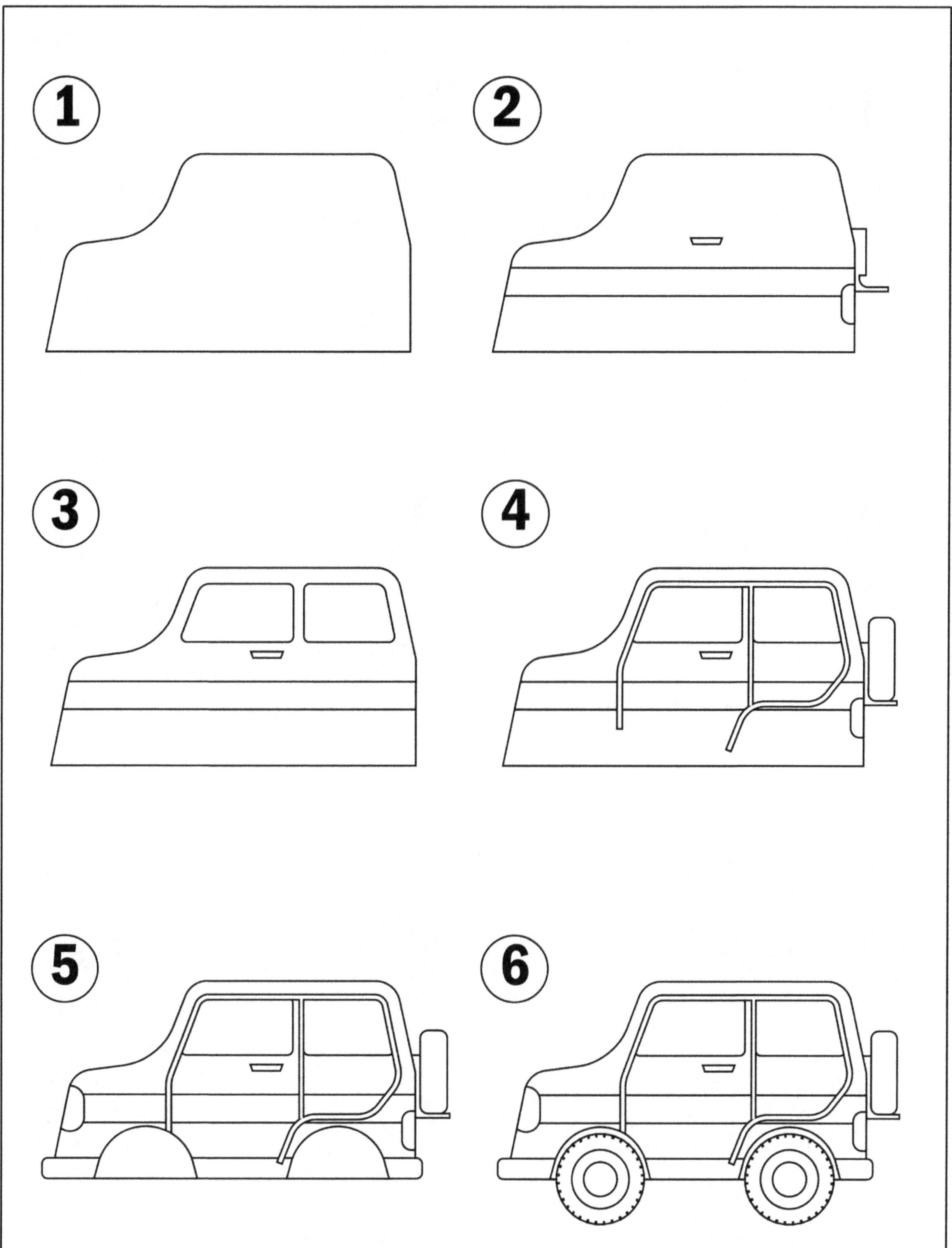

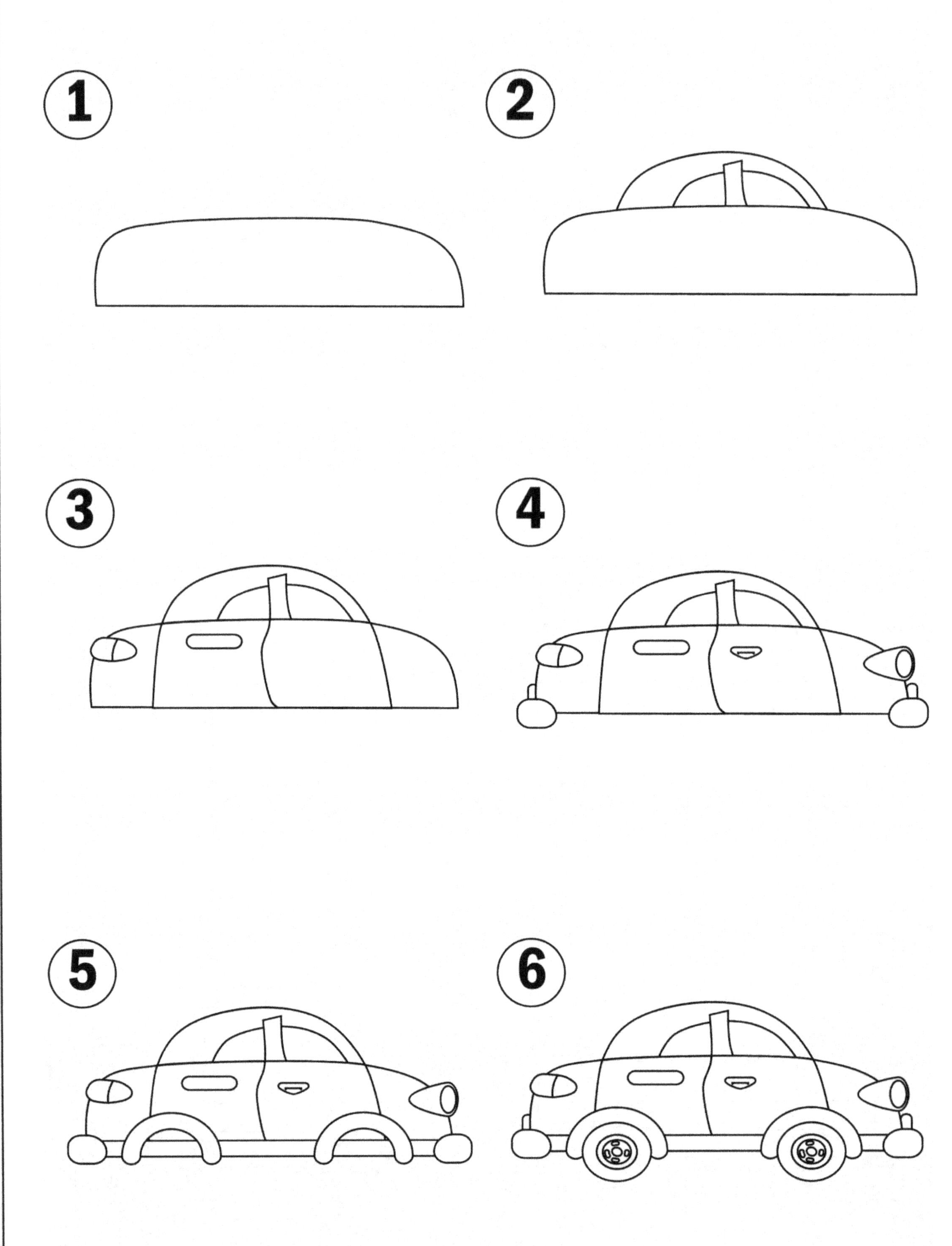

1
2
3
4
5
6

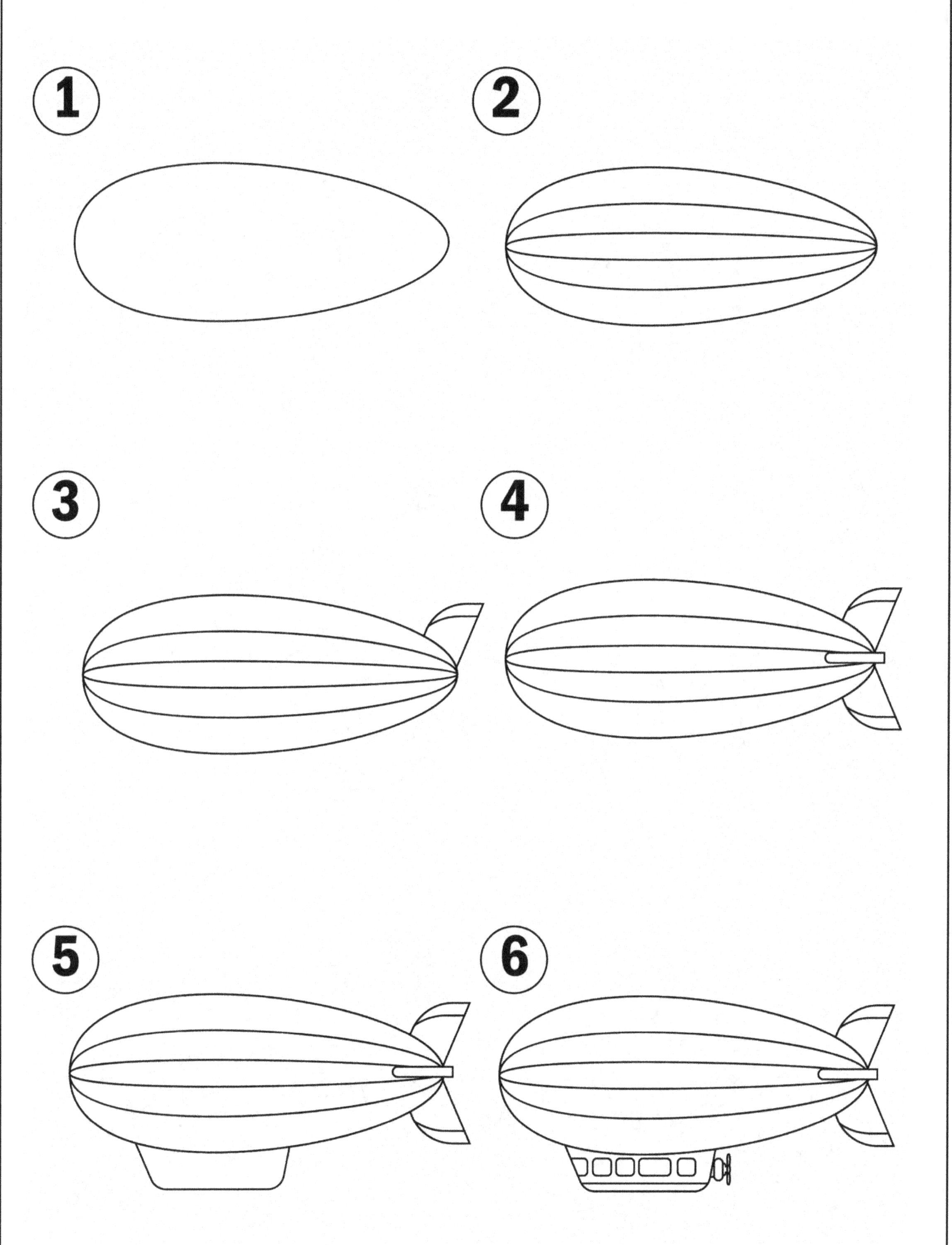

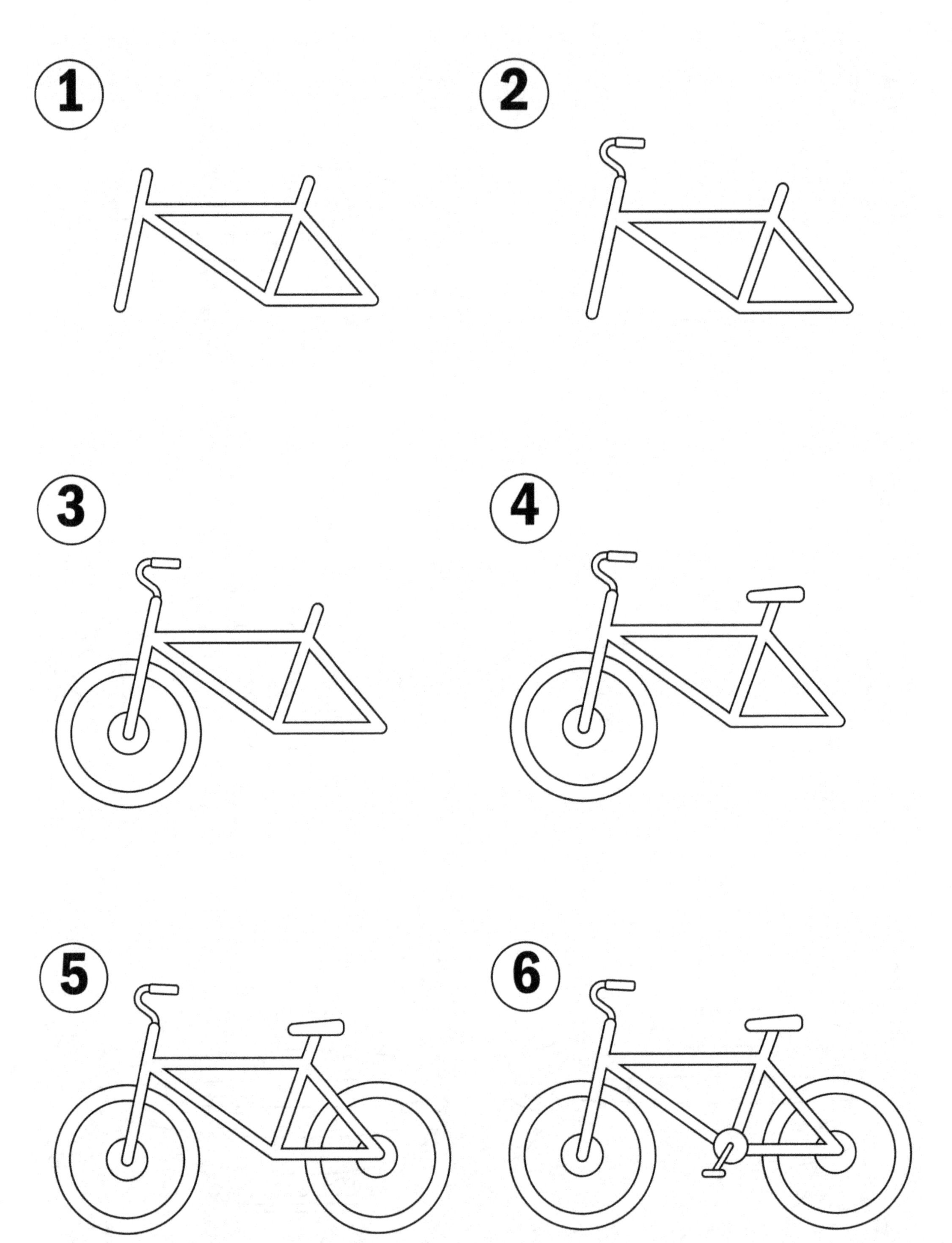

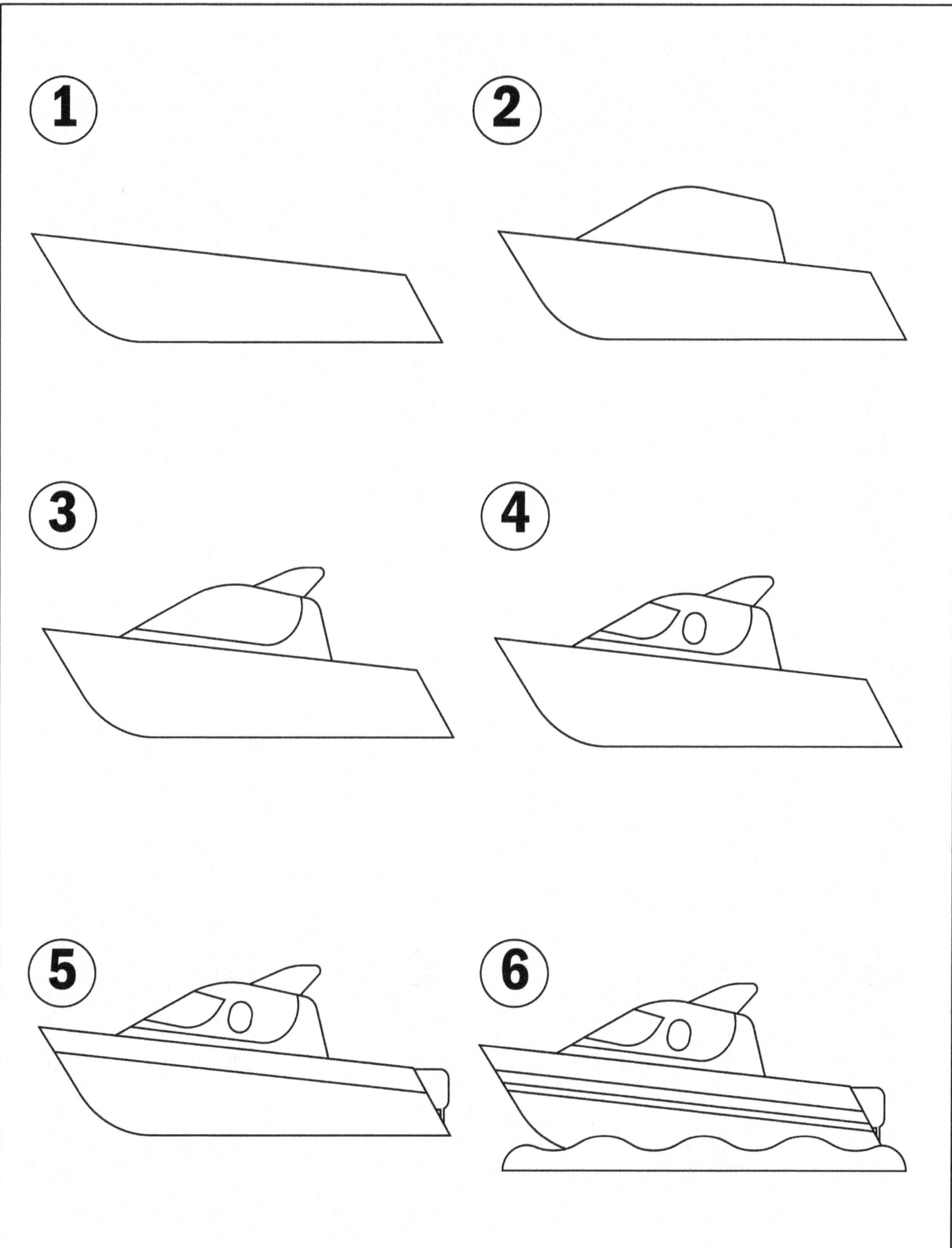

1
2
3
4
5
6

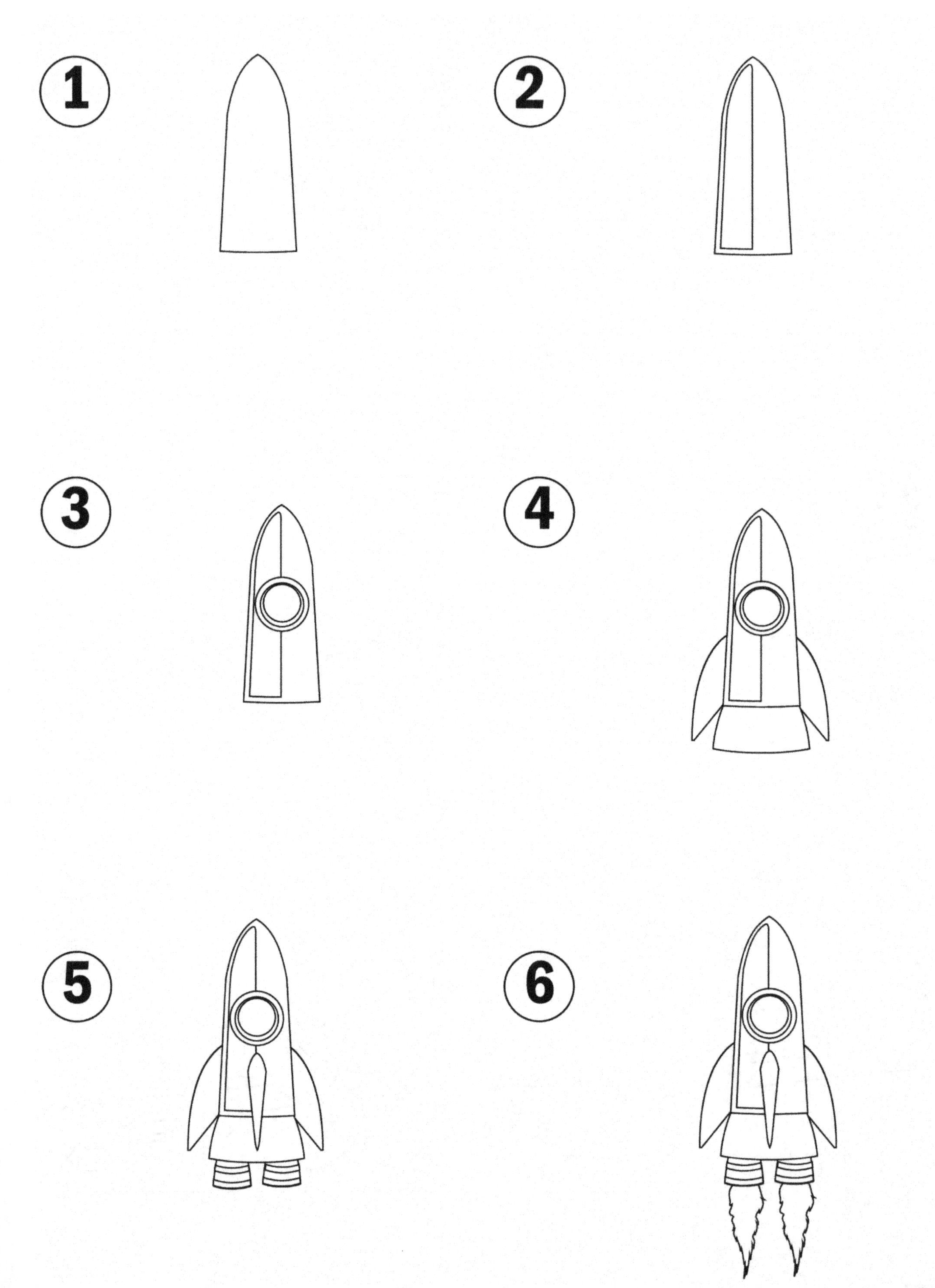

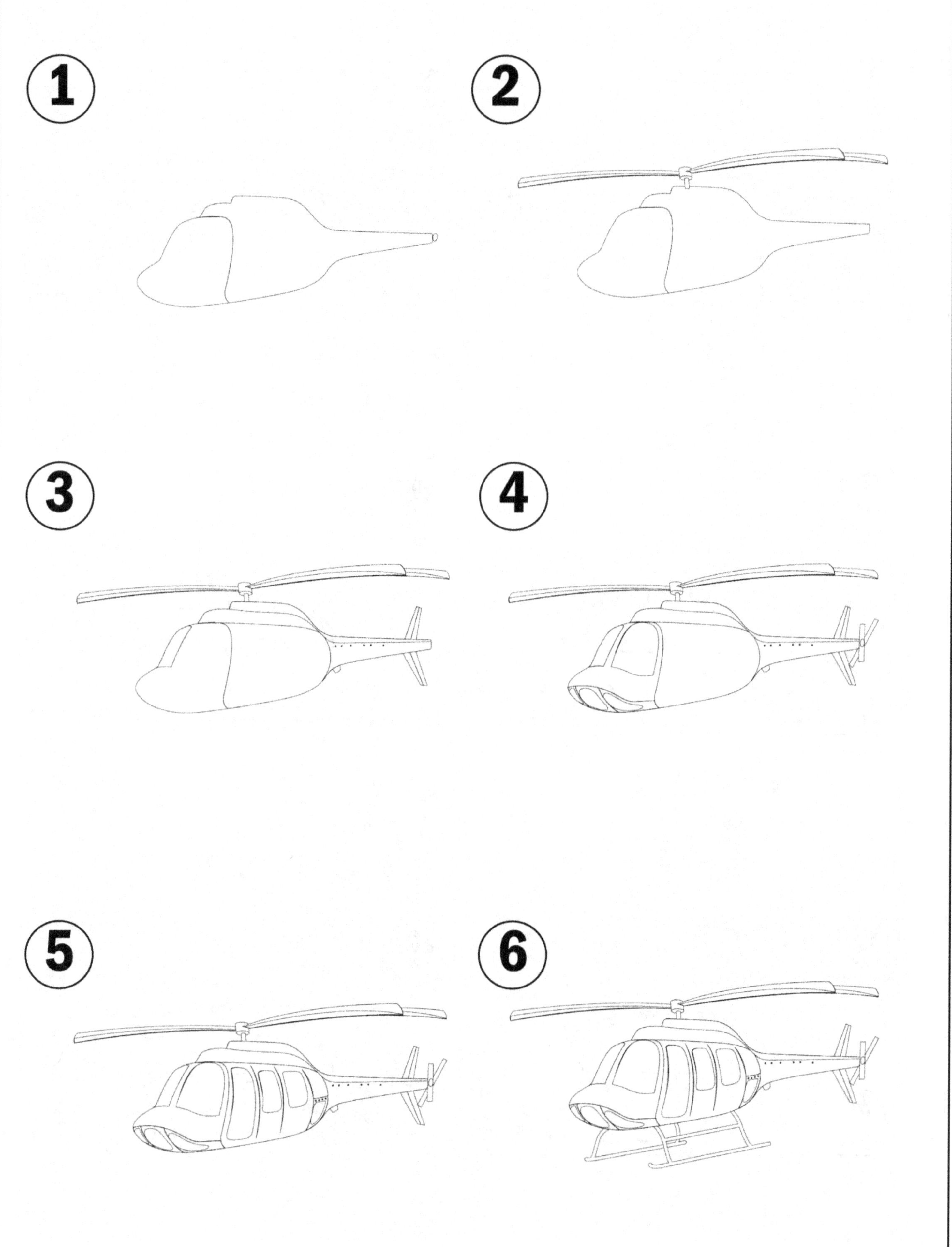

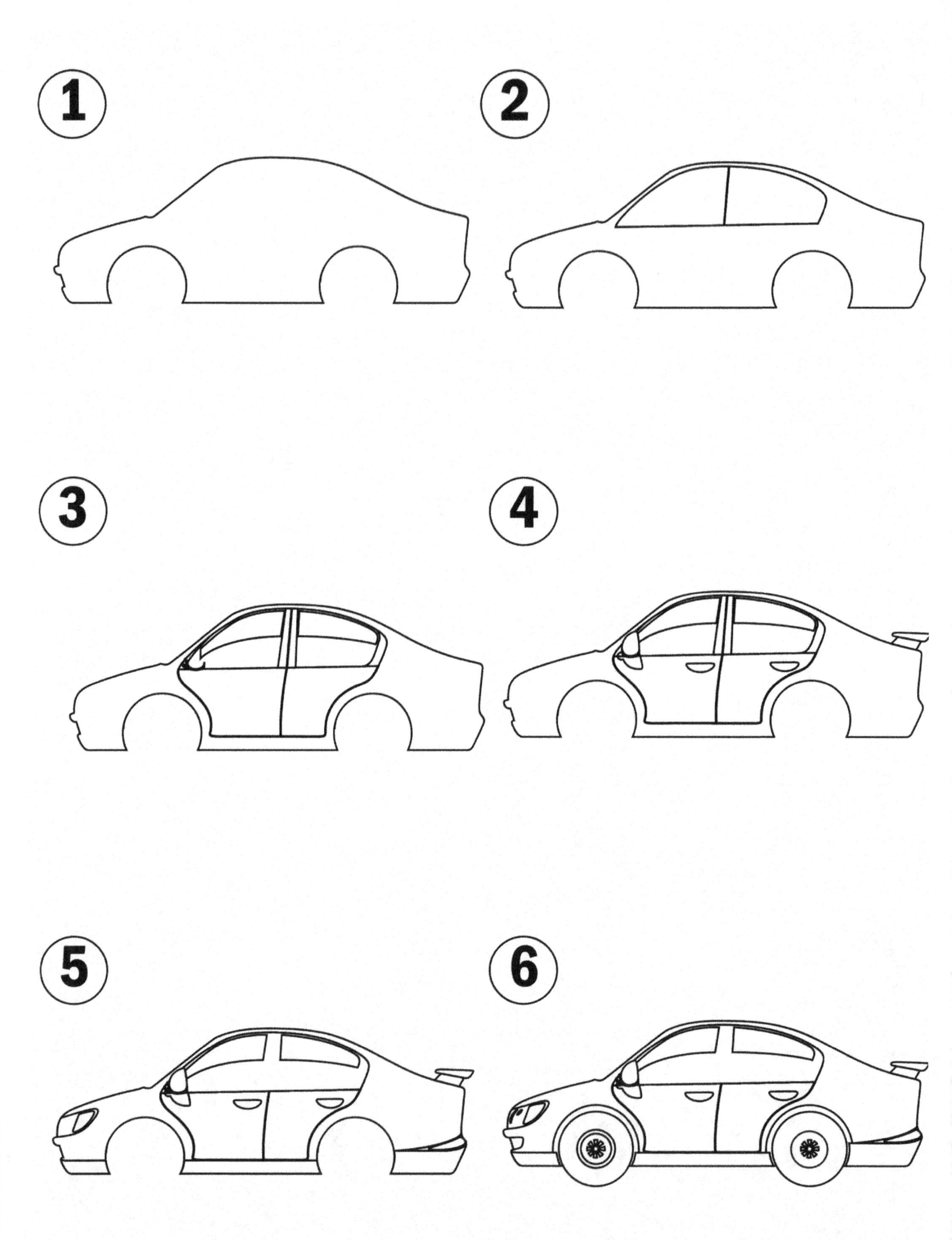

1
2
3
4
5
6

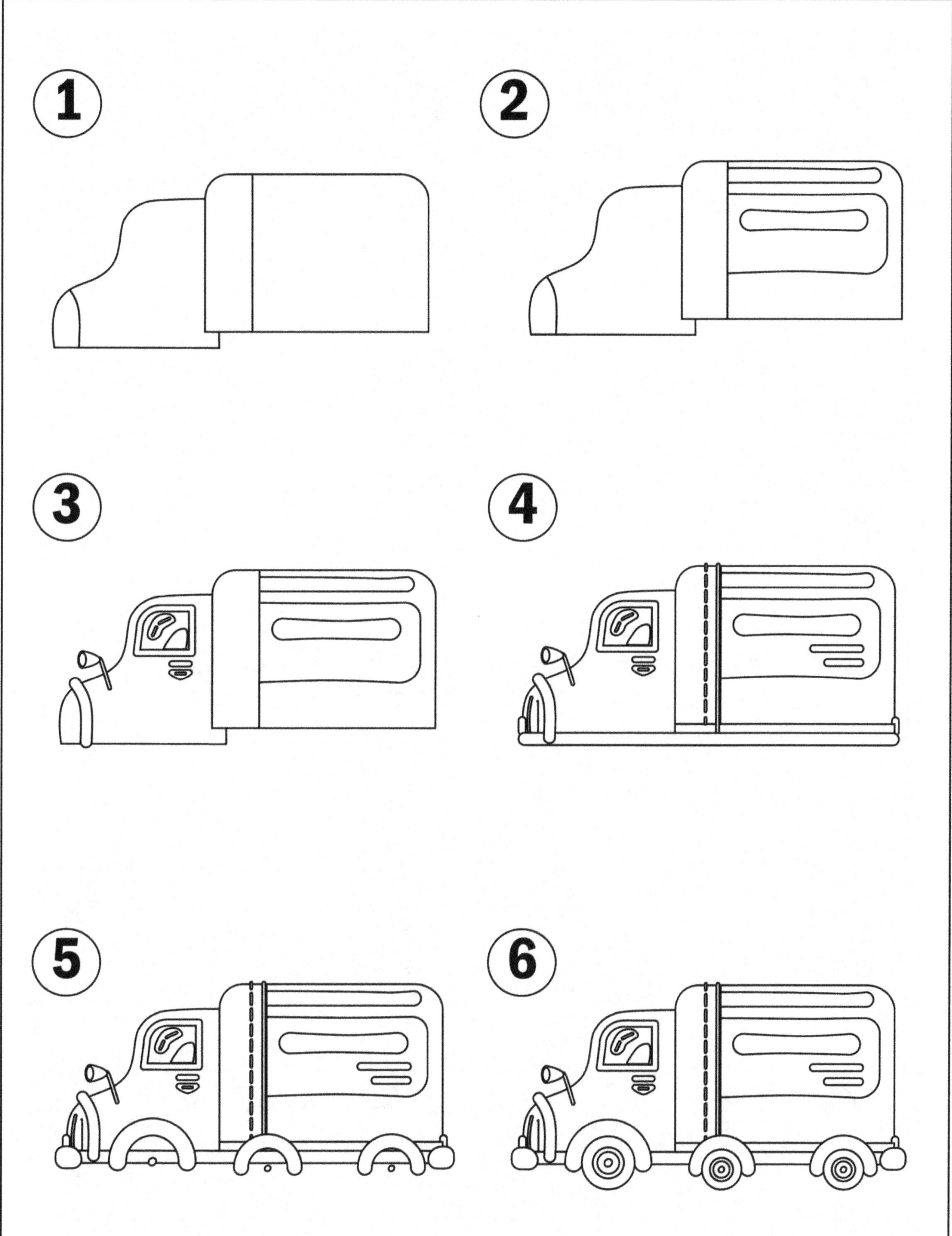

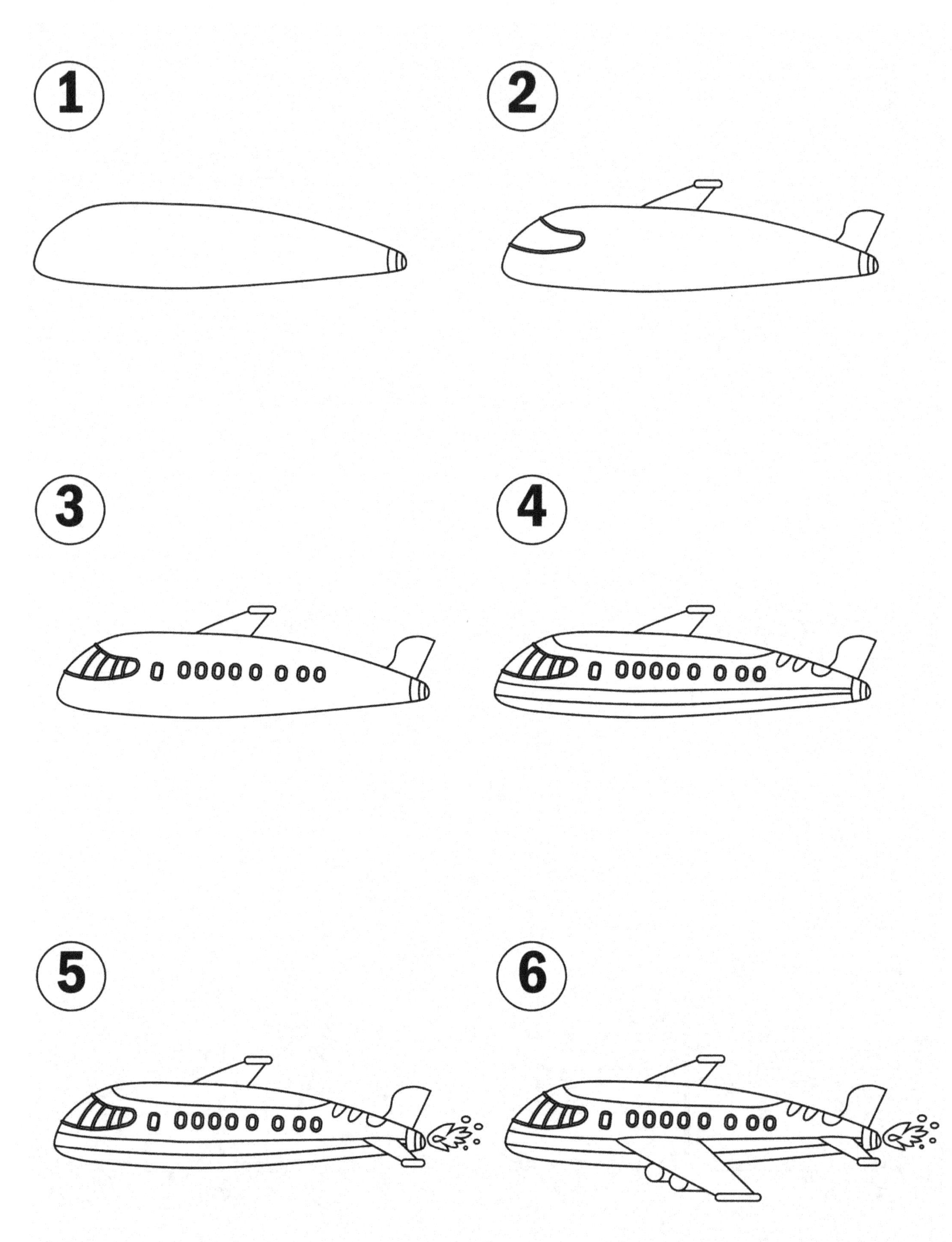

1
2
3
4
5
6

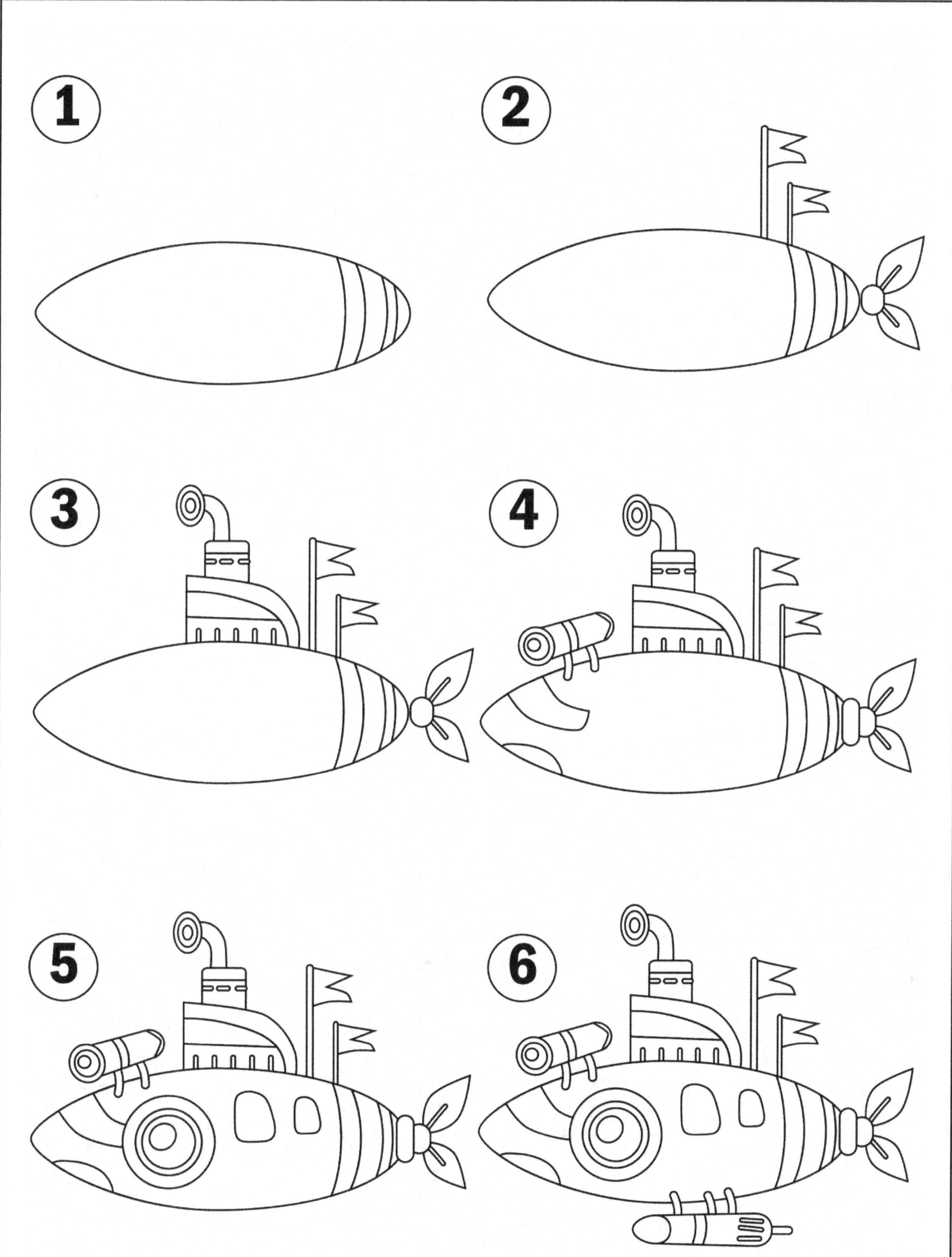

1
2
3
4
5
6

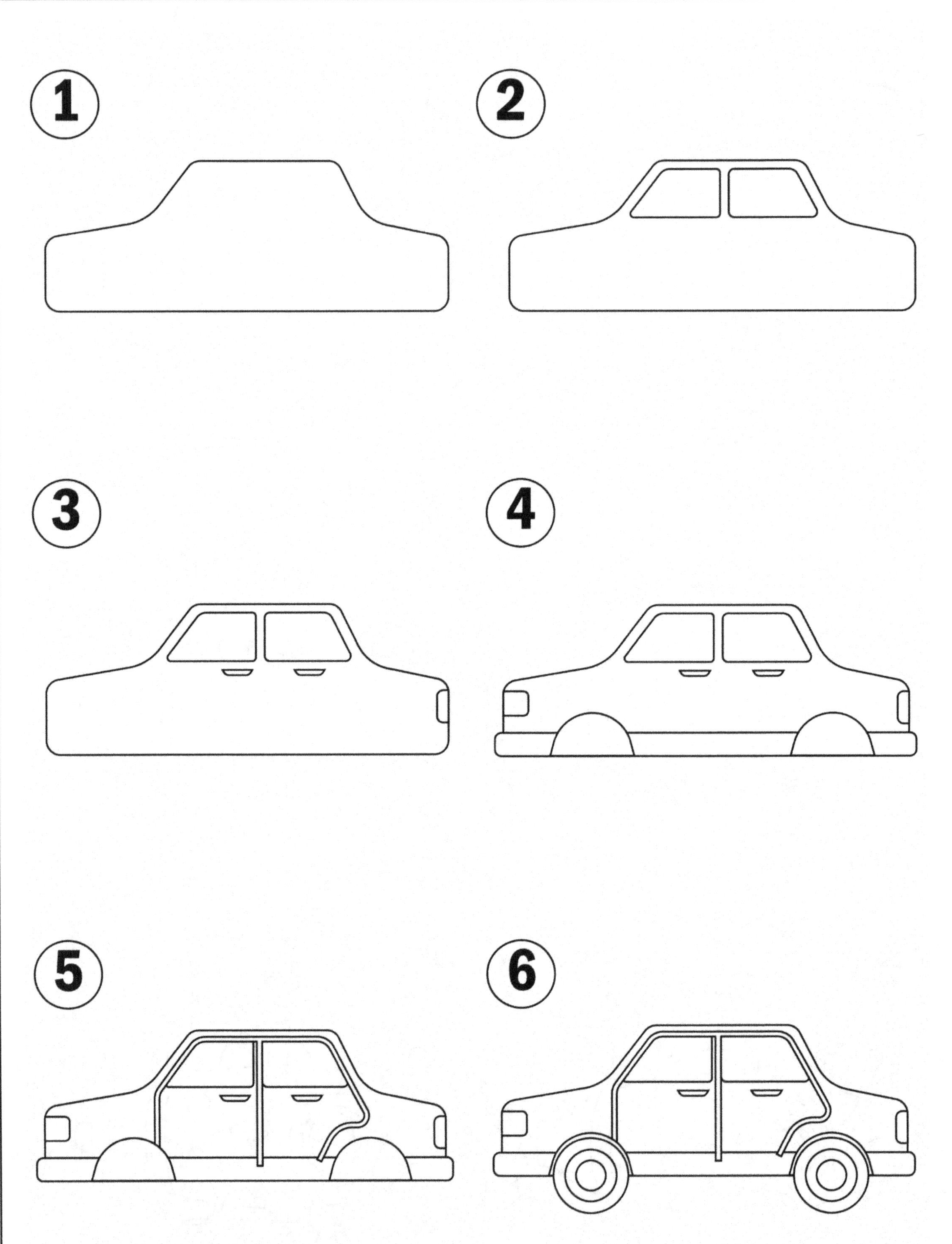

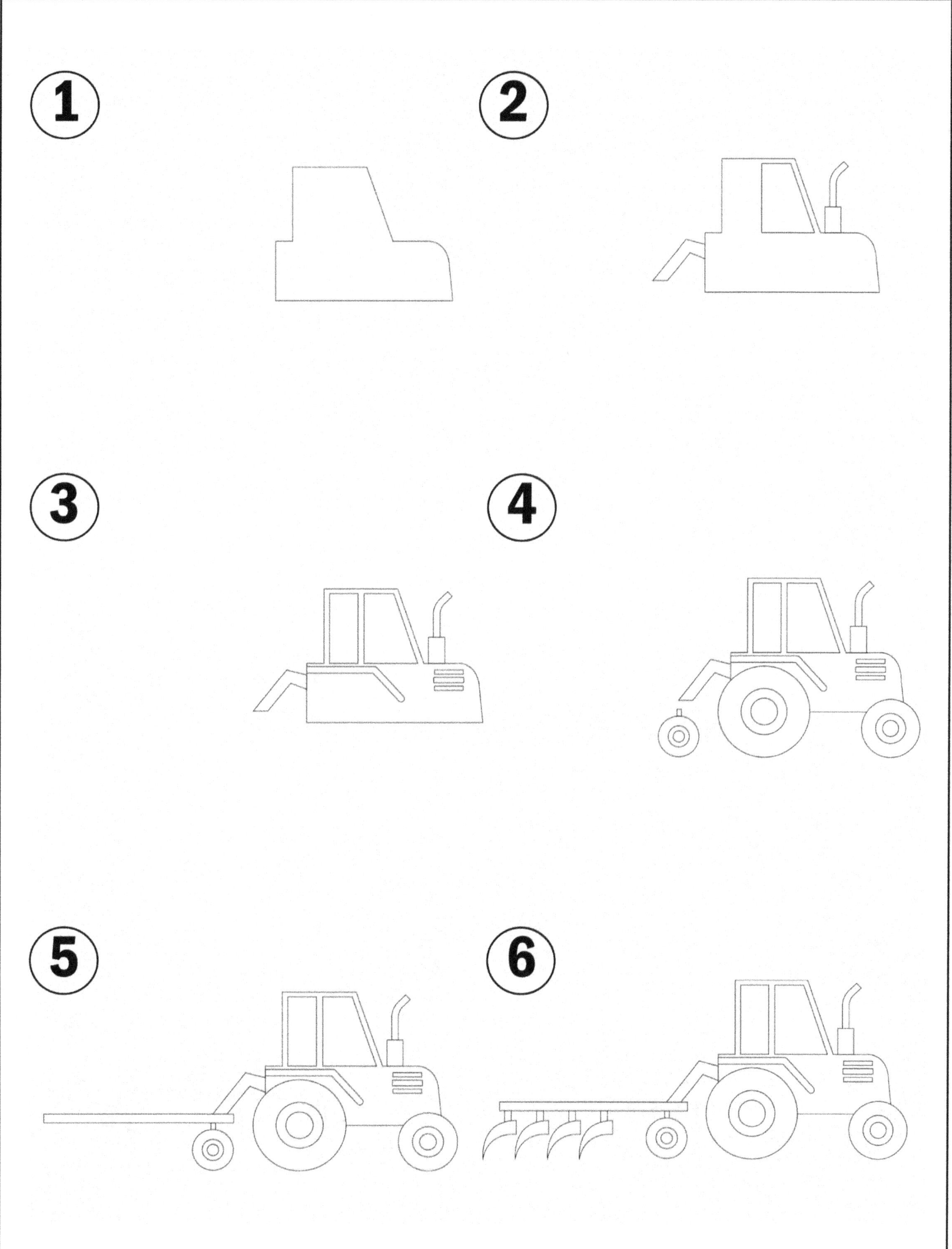

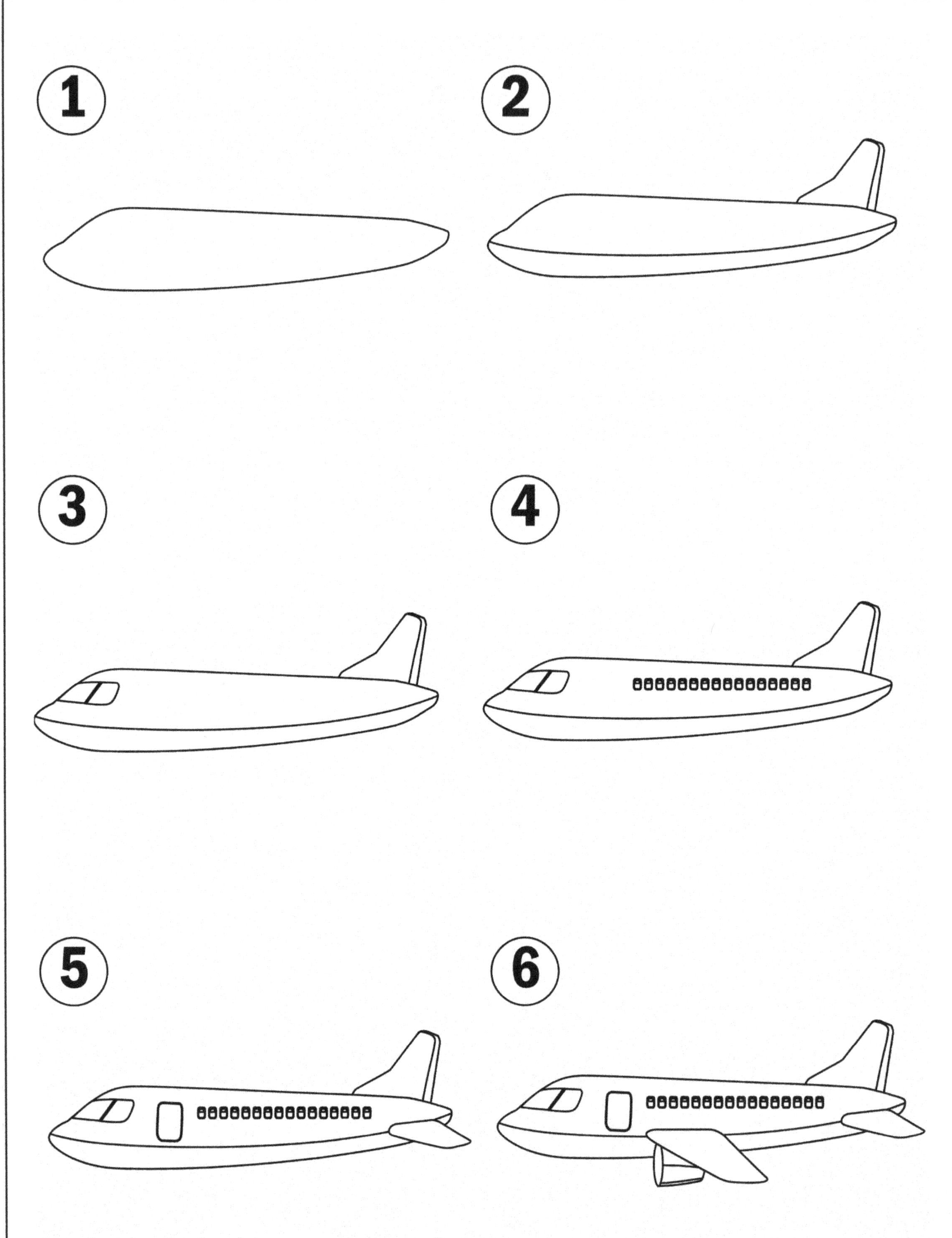

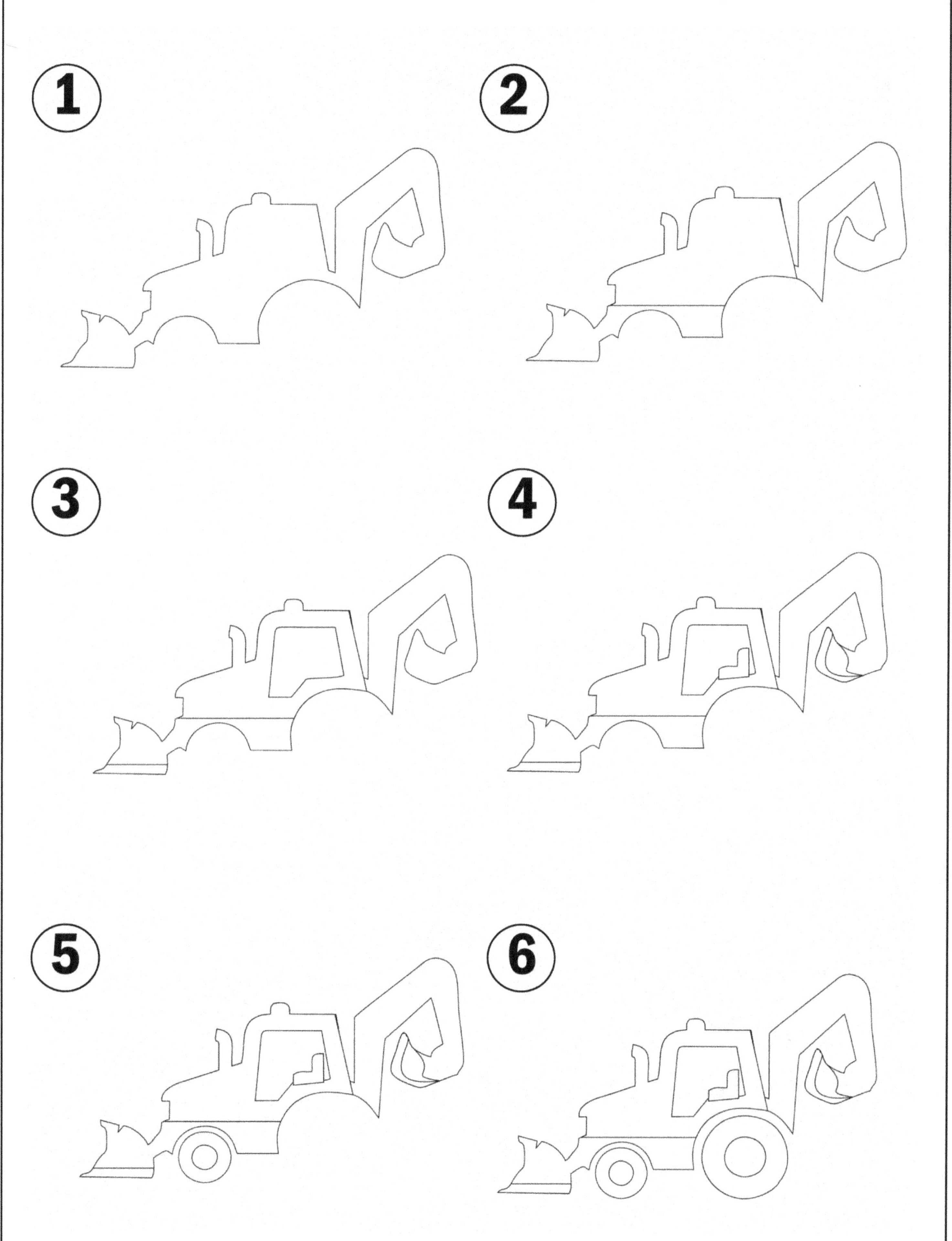

1
2
3
4
5
6

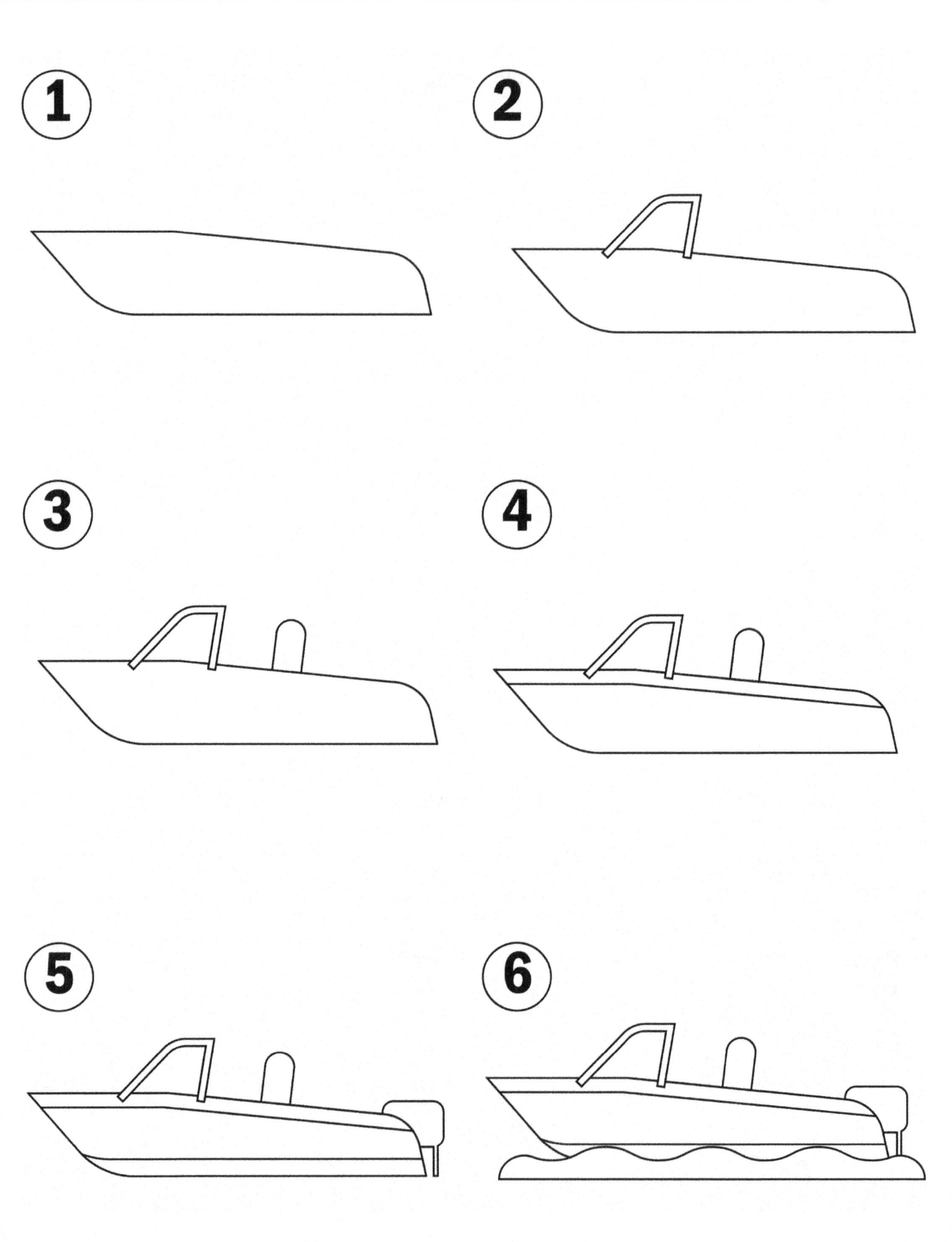

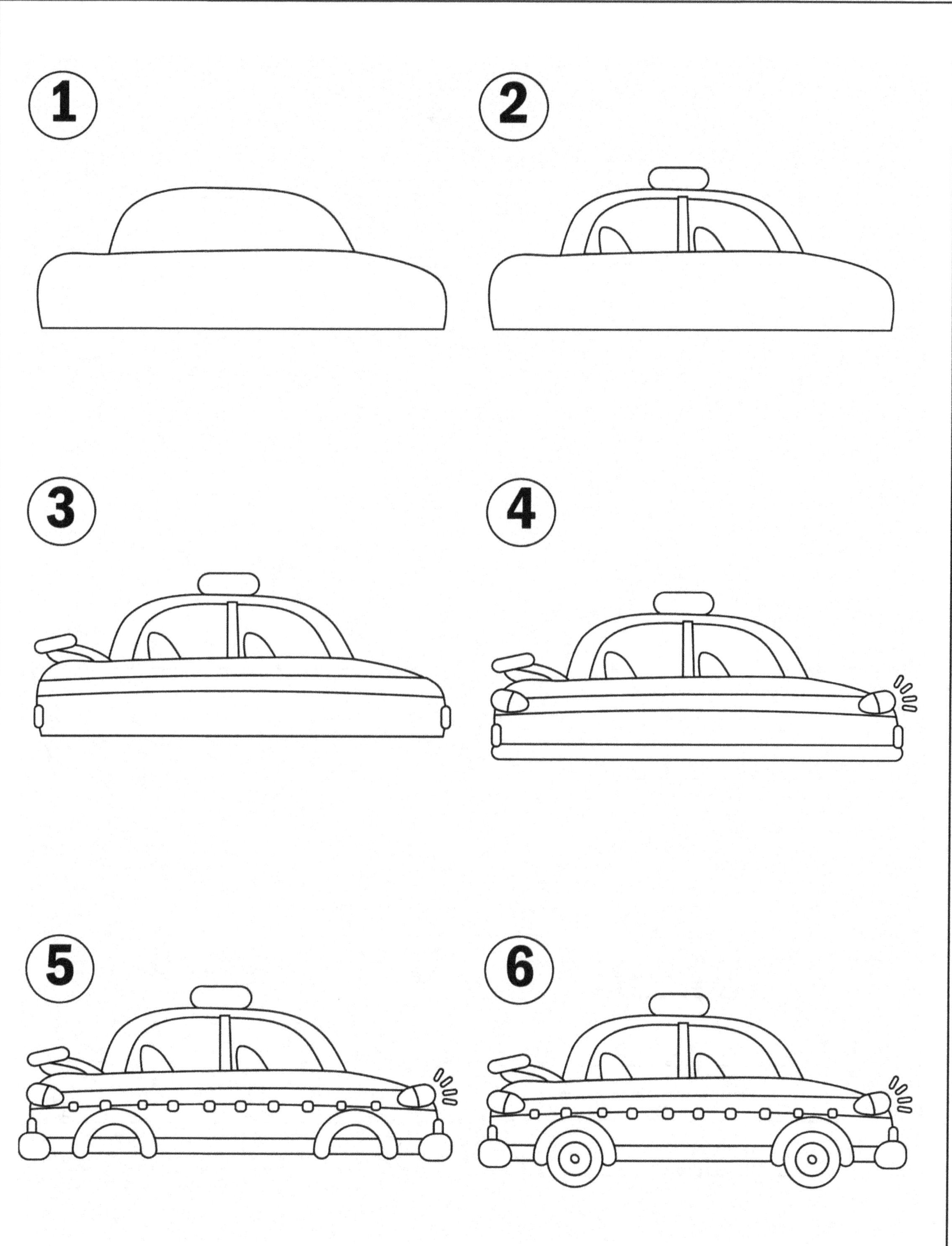

1
2
3
4
5
6

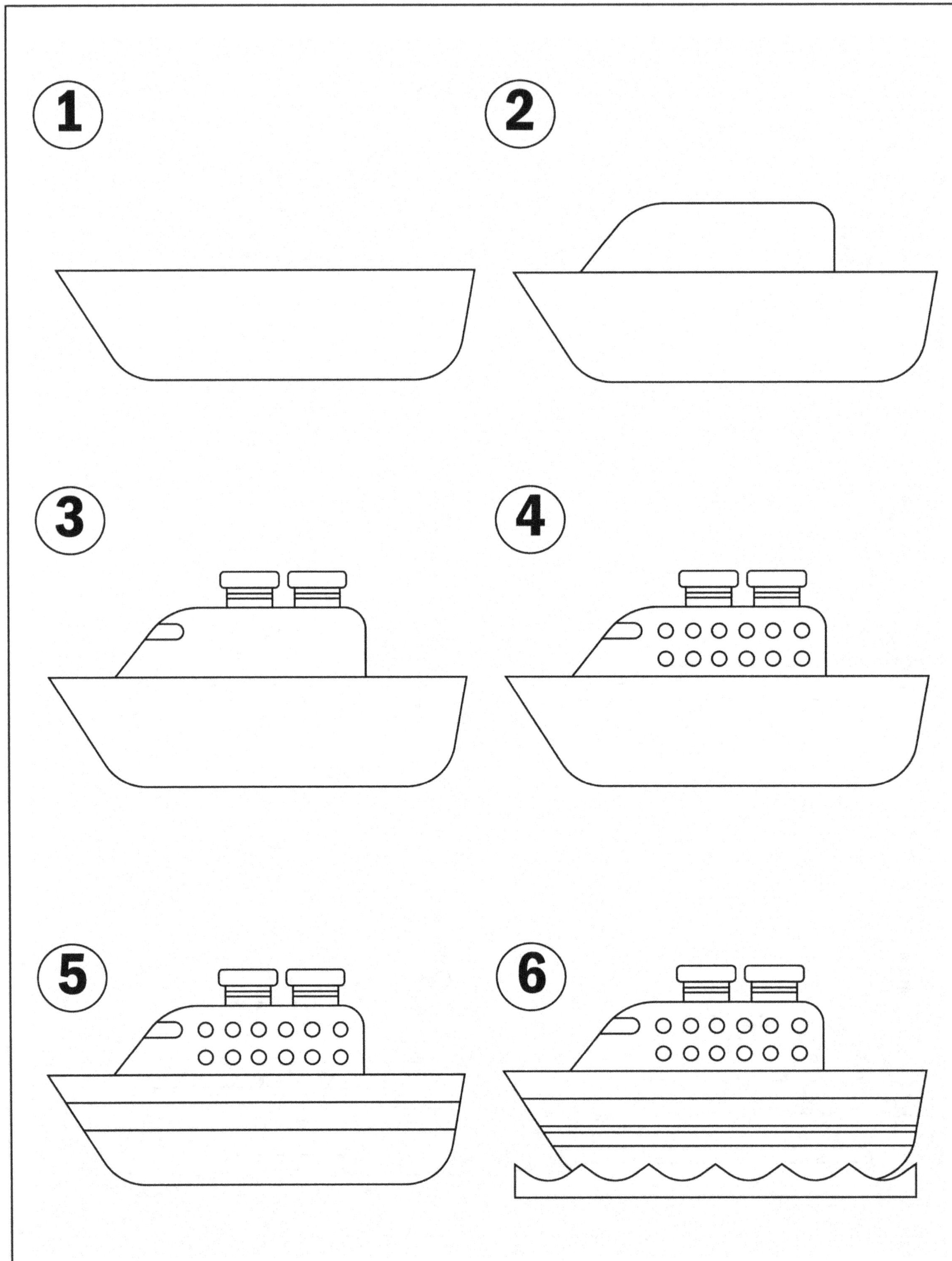

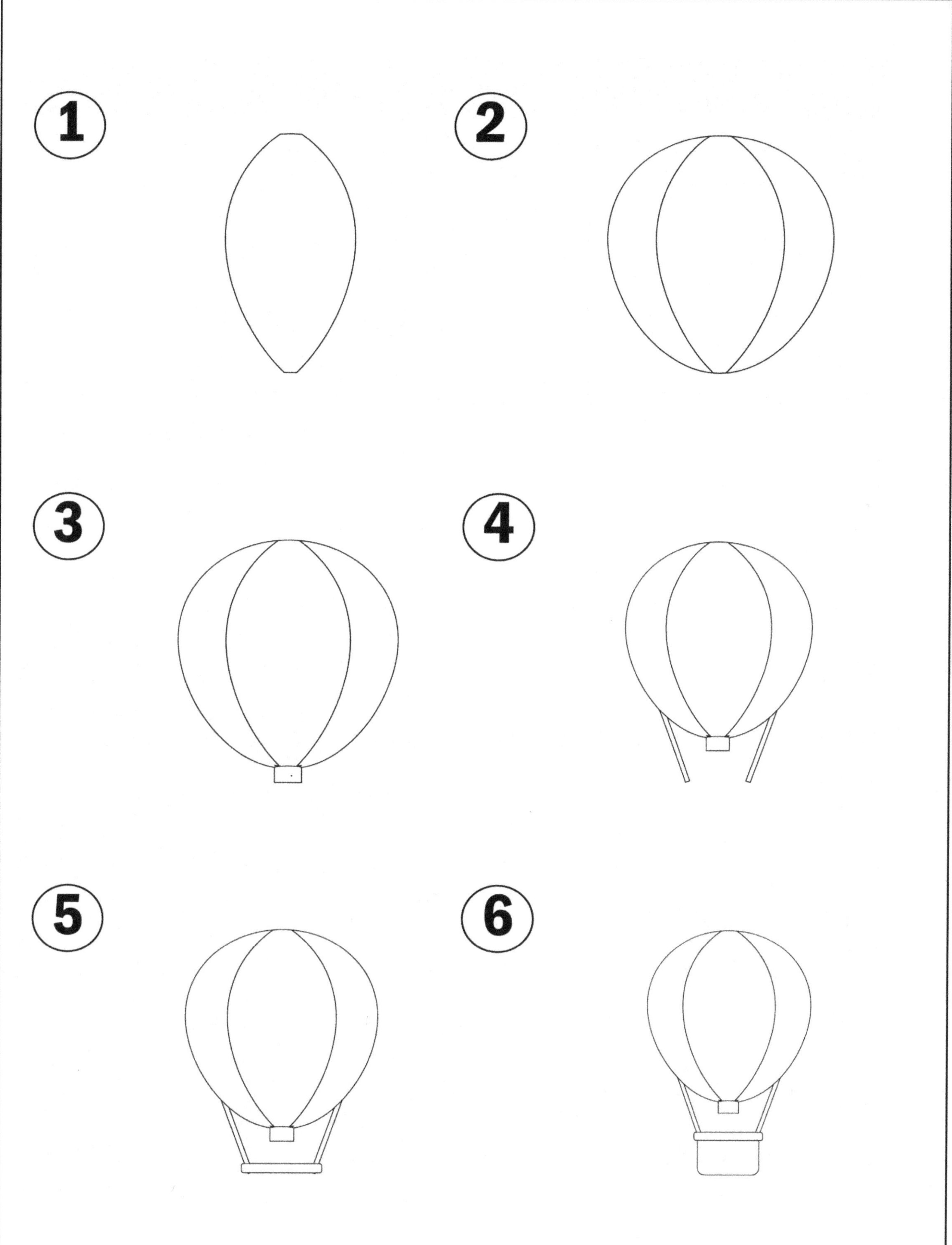

1
2
3
4
5
6

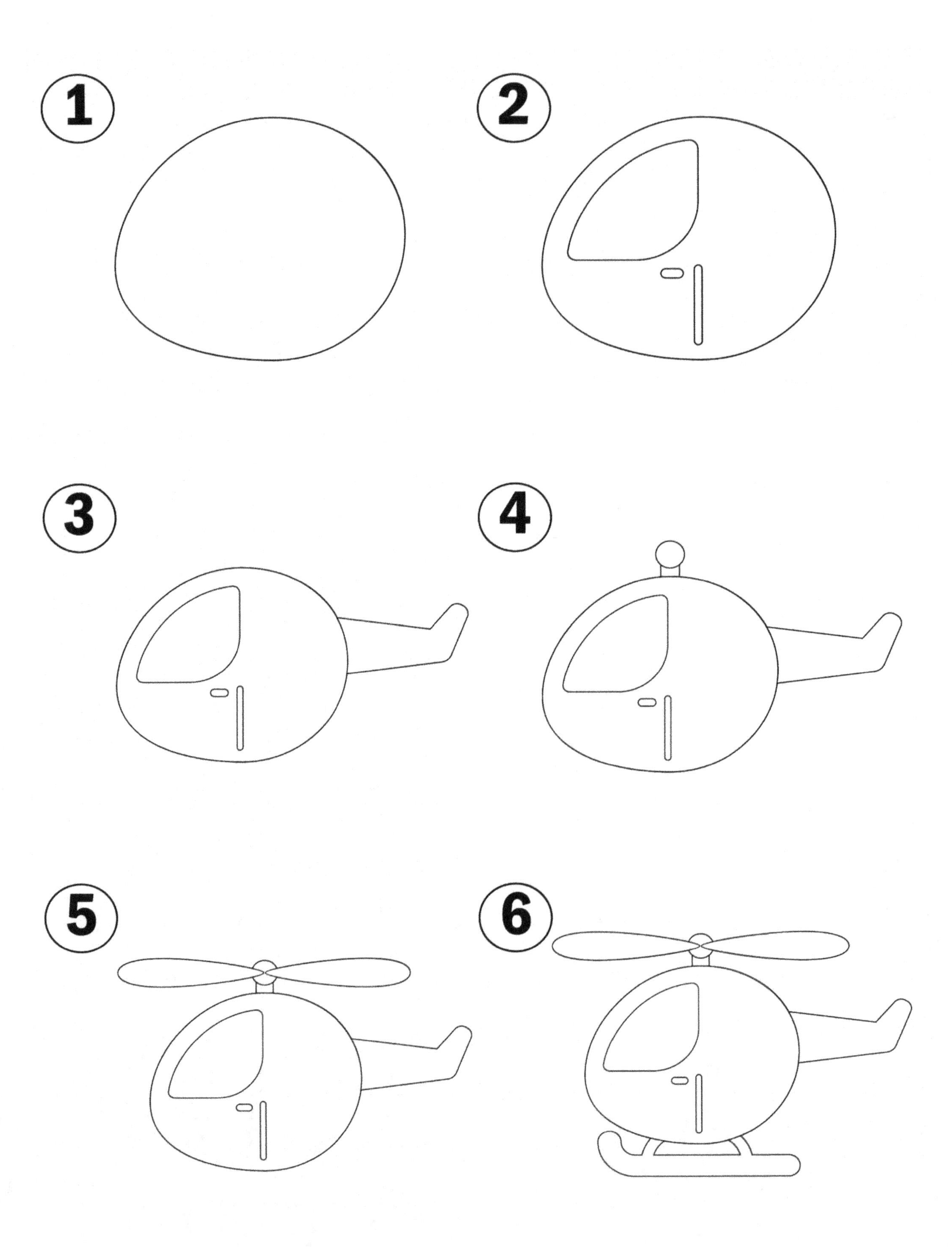

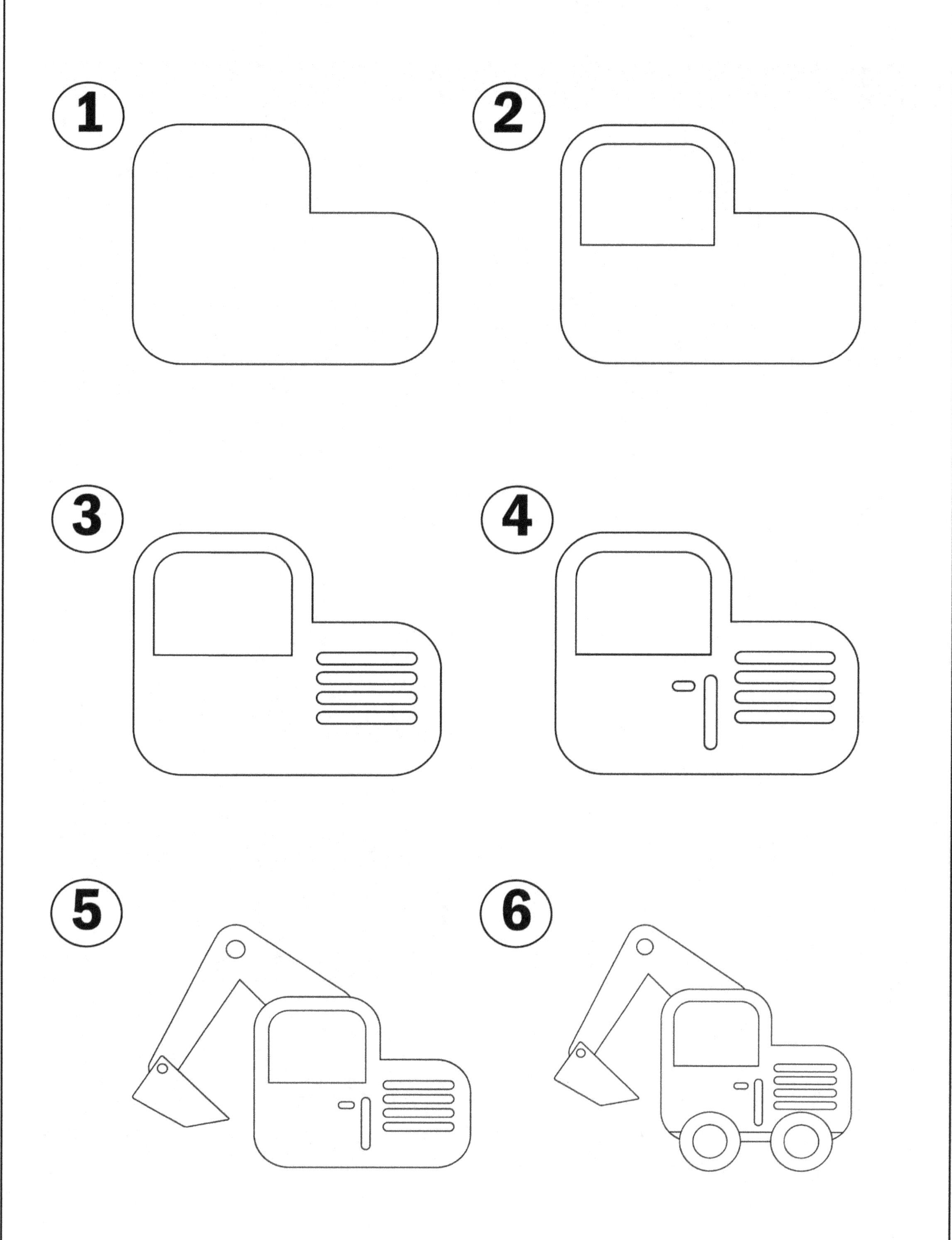

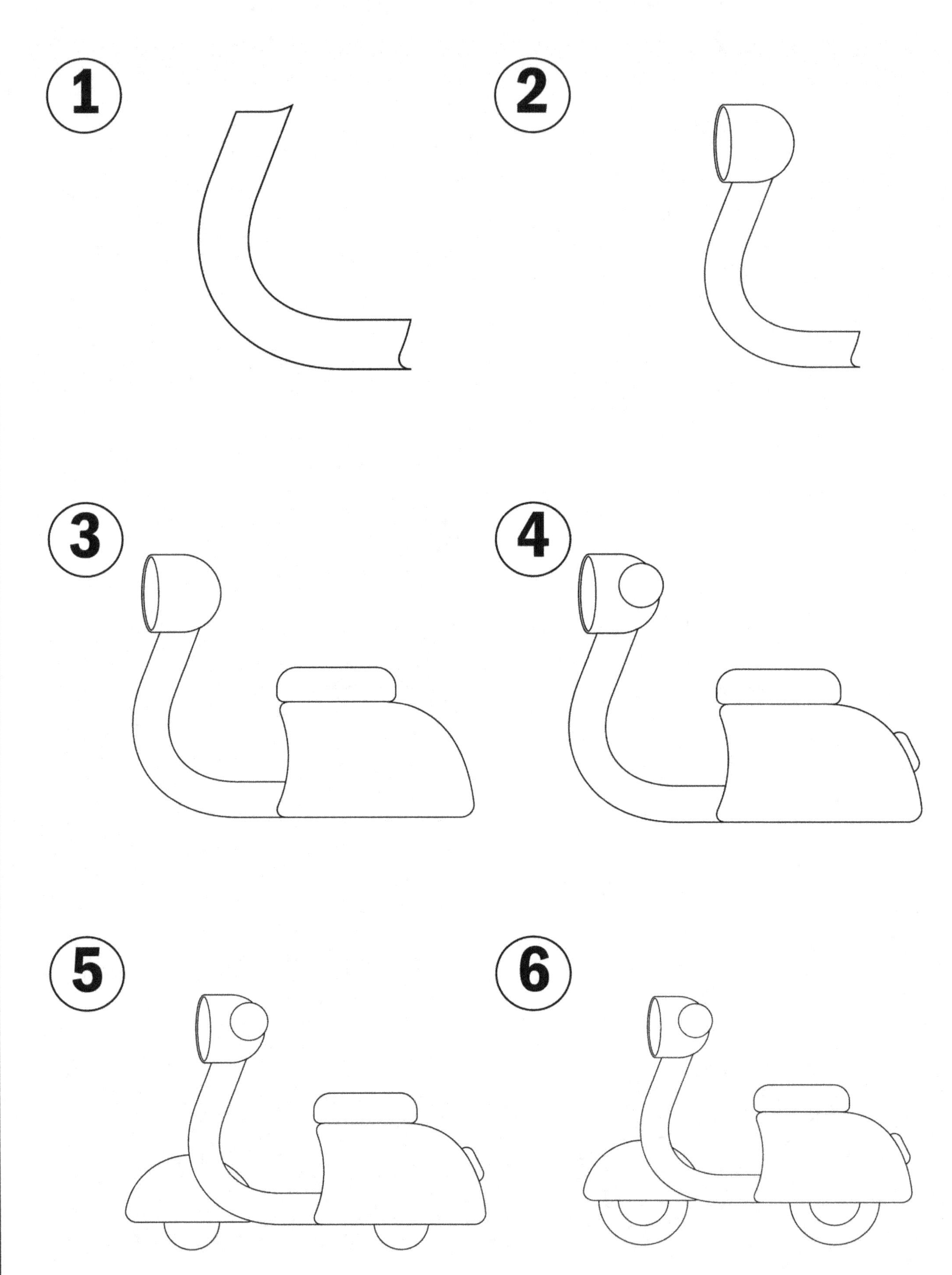

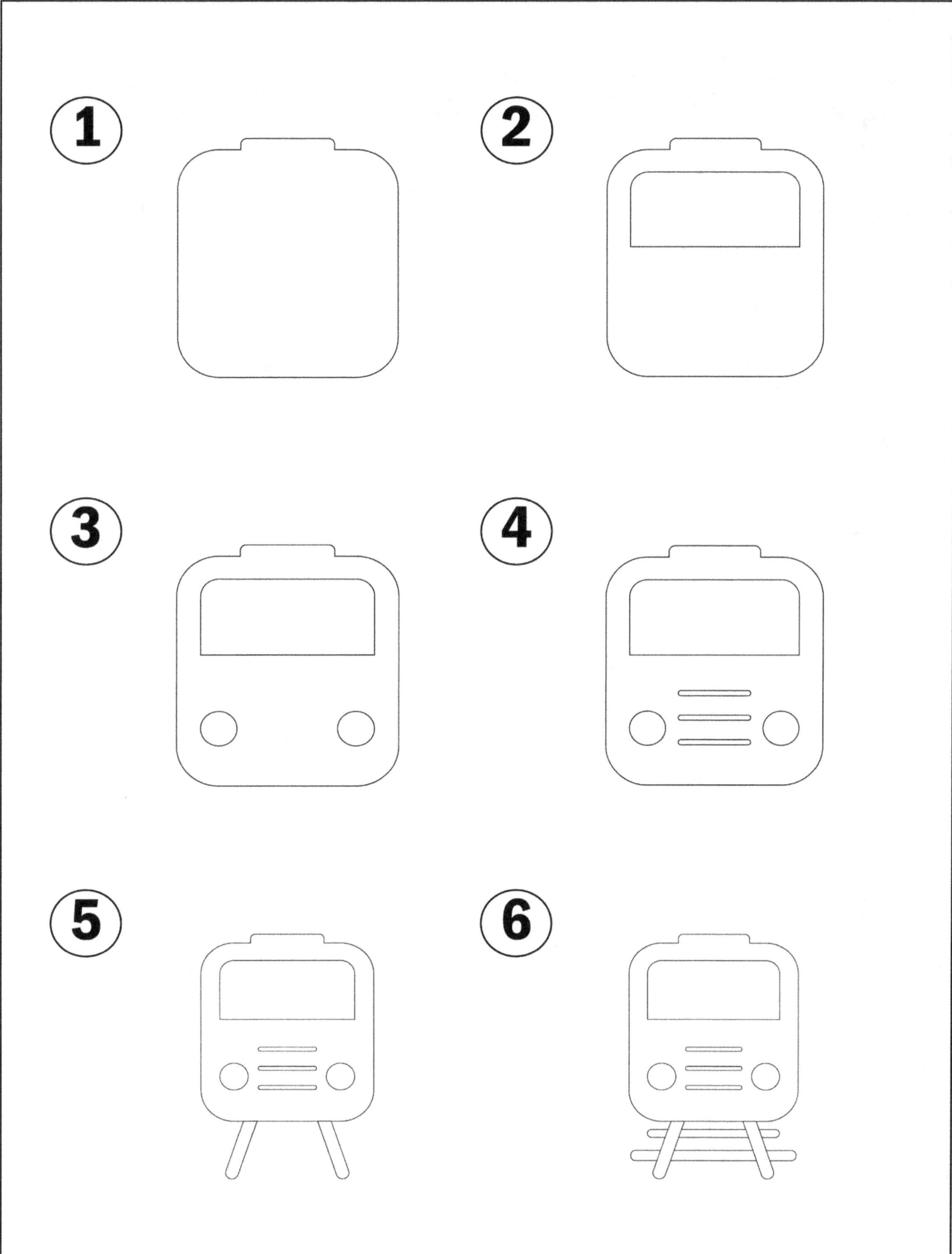

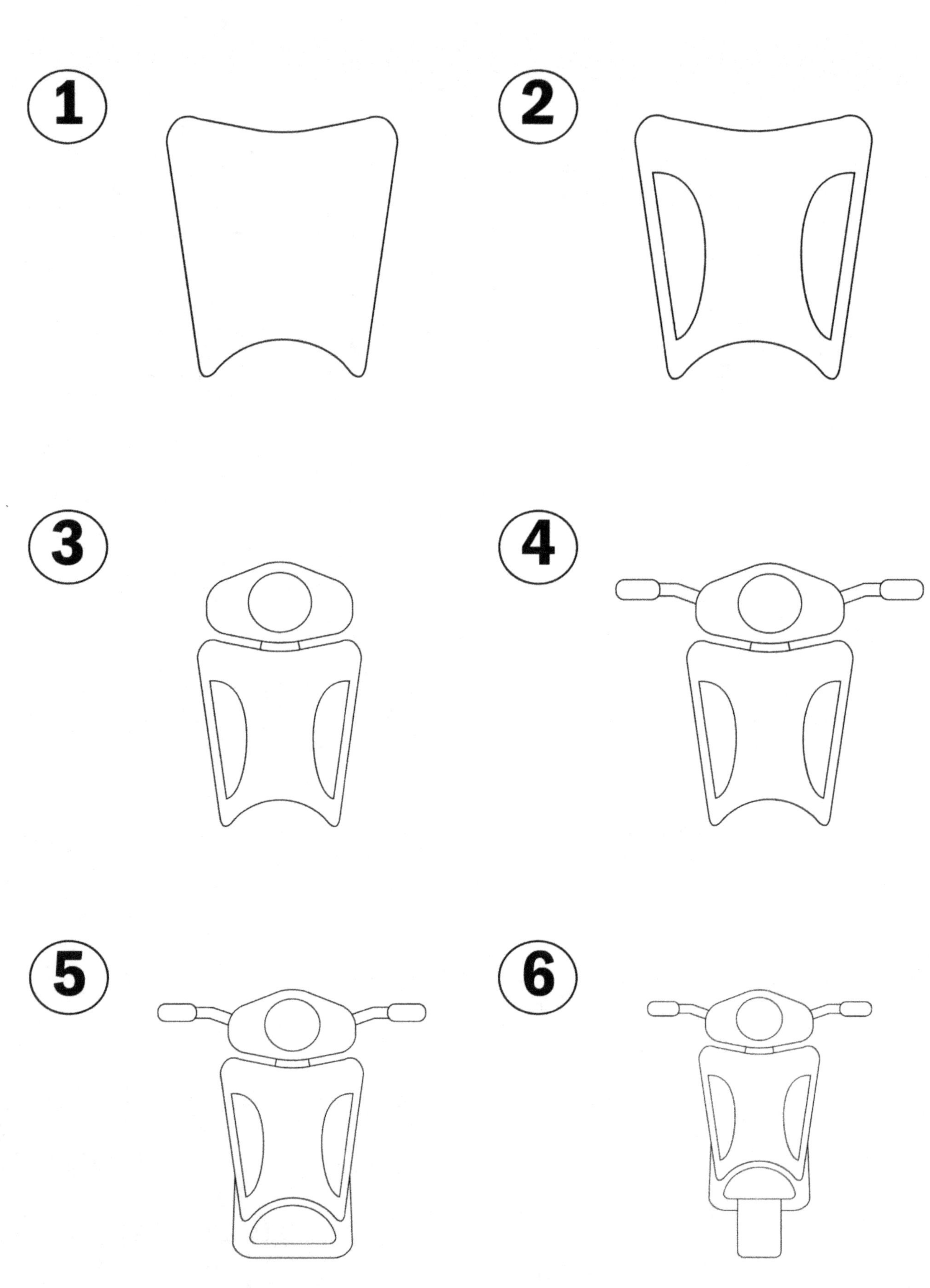

1
2
3
4
5
6

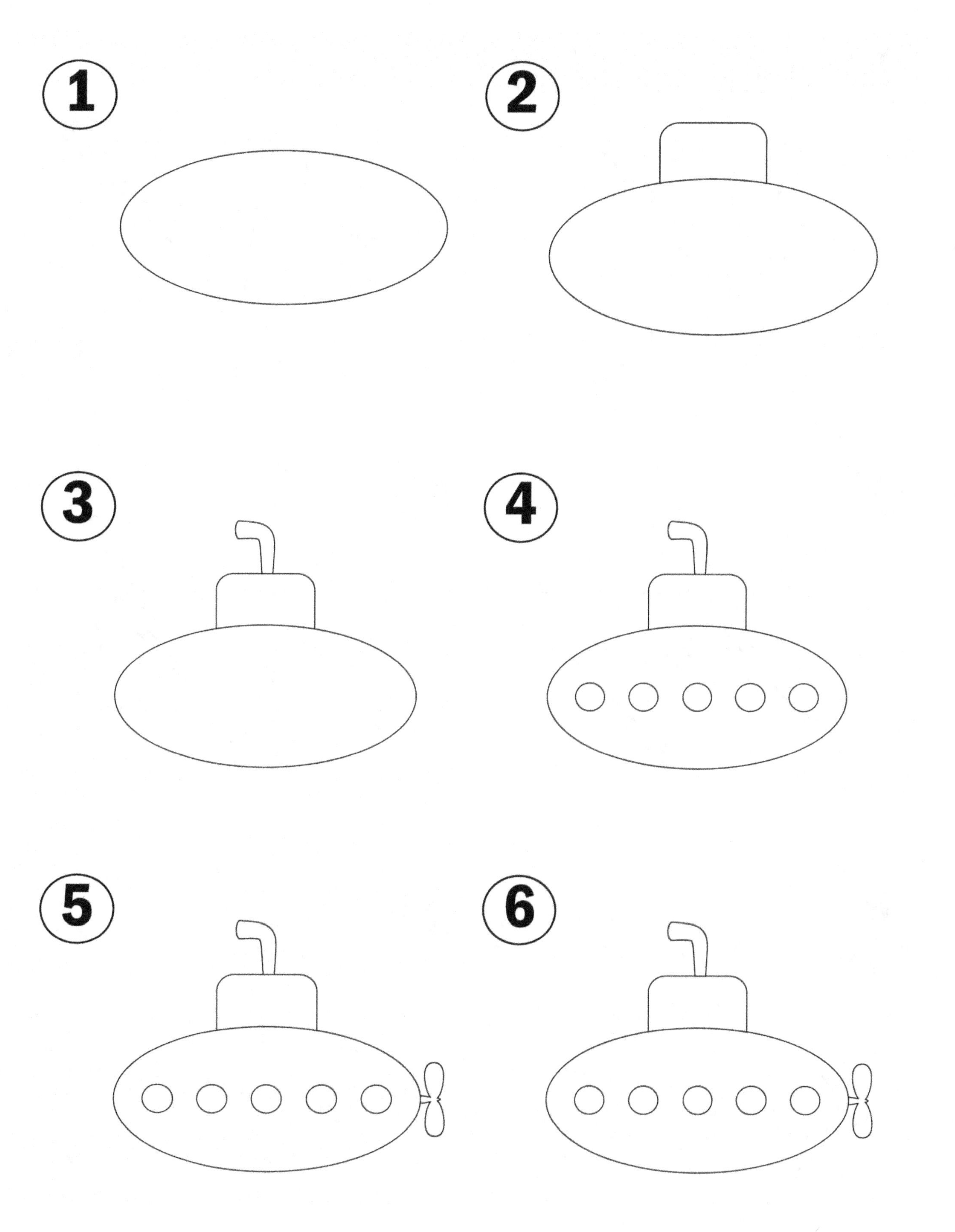

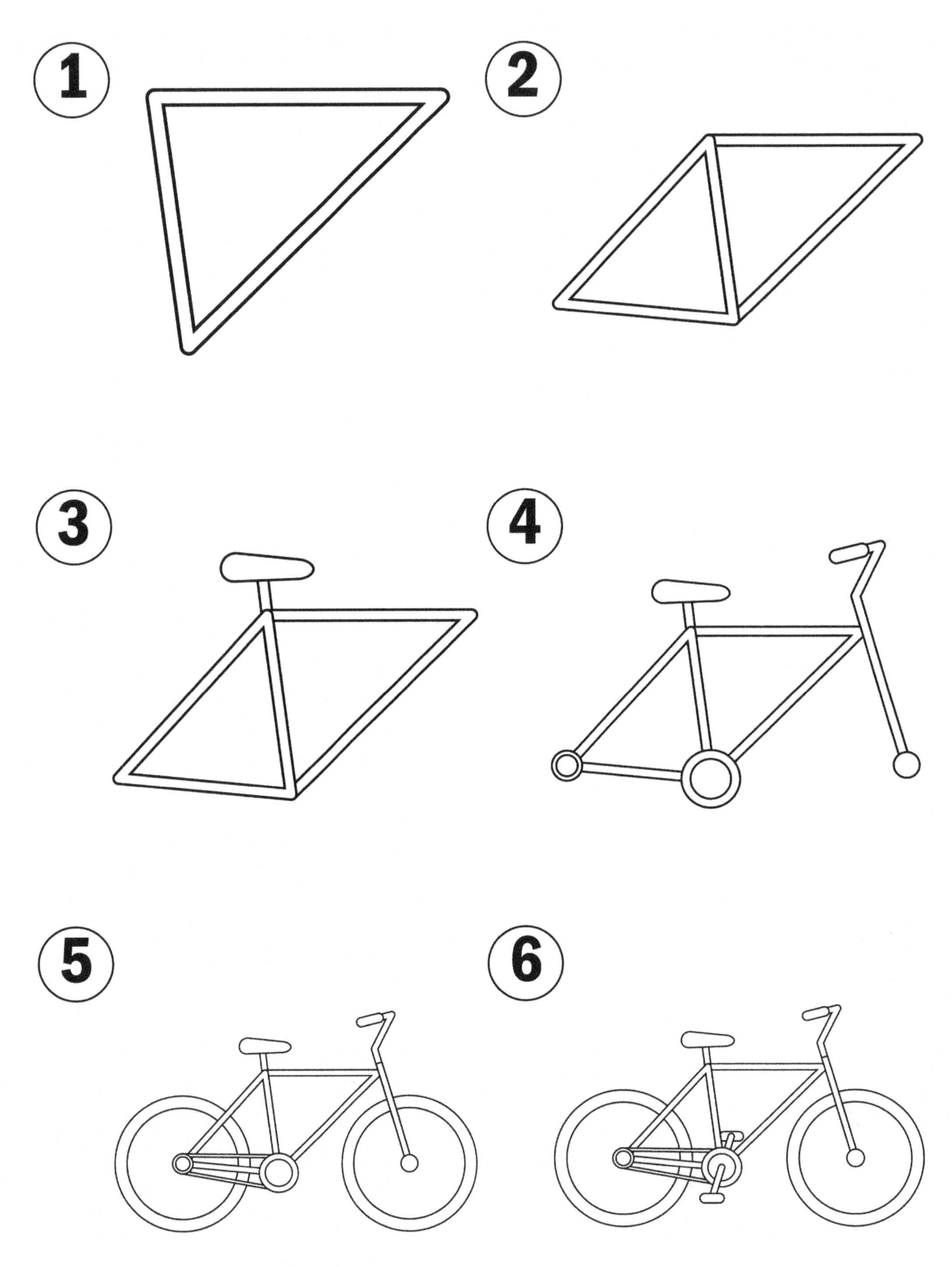

1
2
3
4
5
6

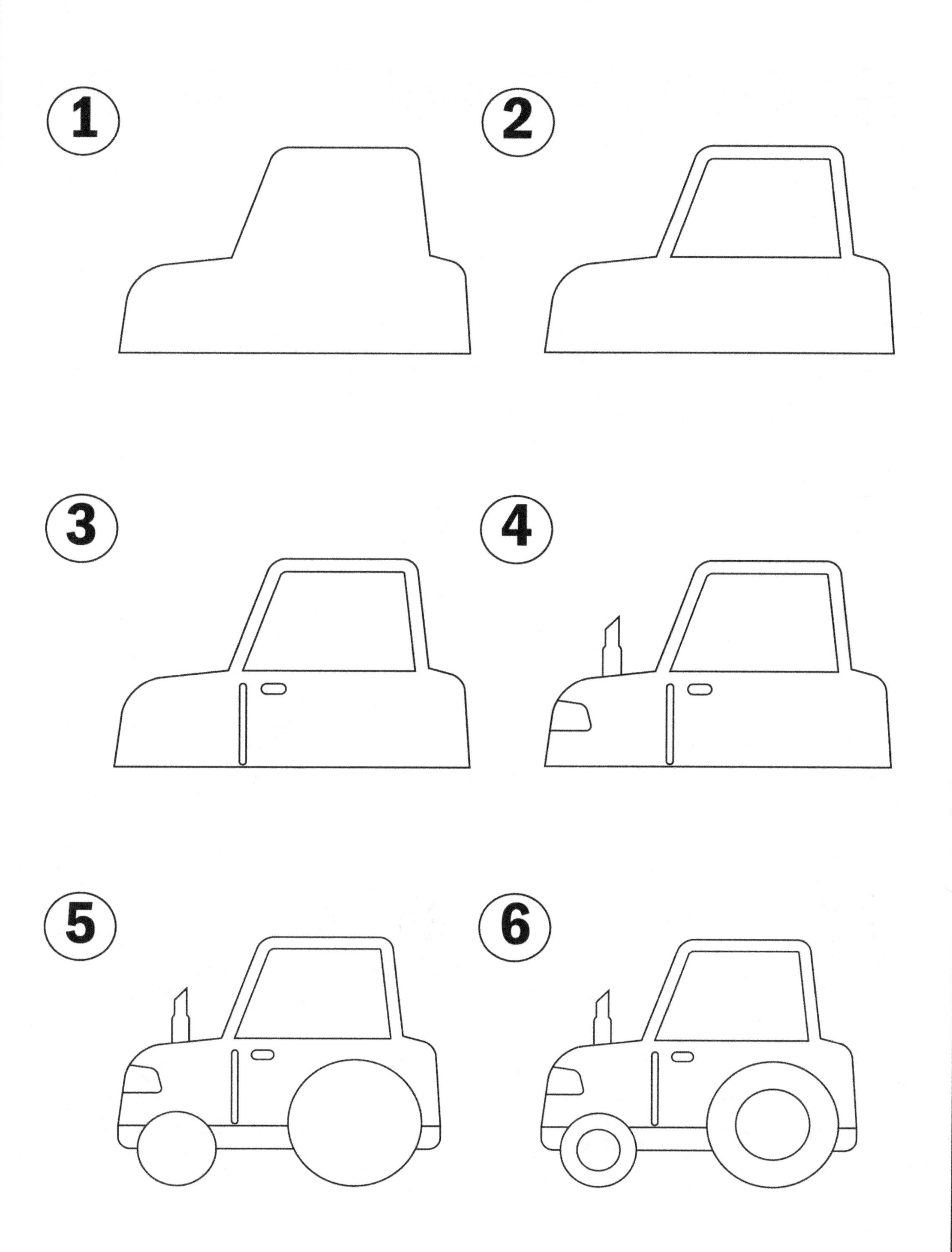
1
2
3
4
5
6

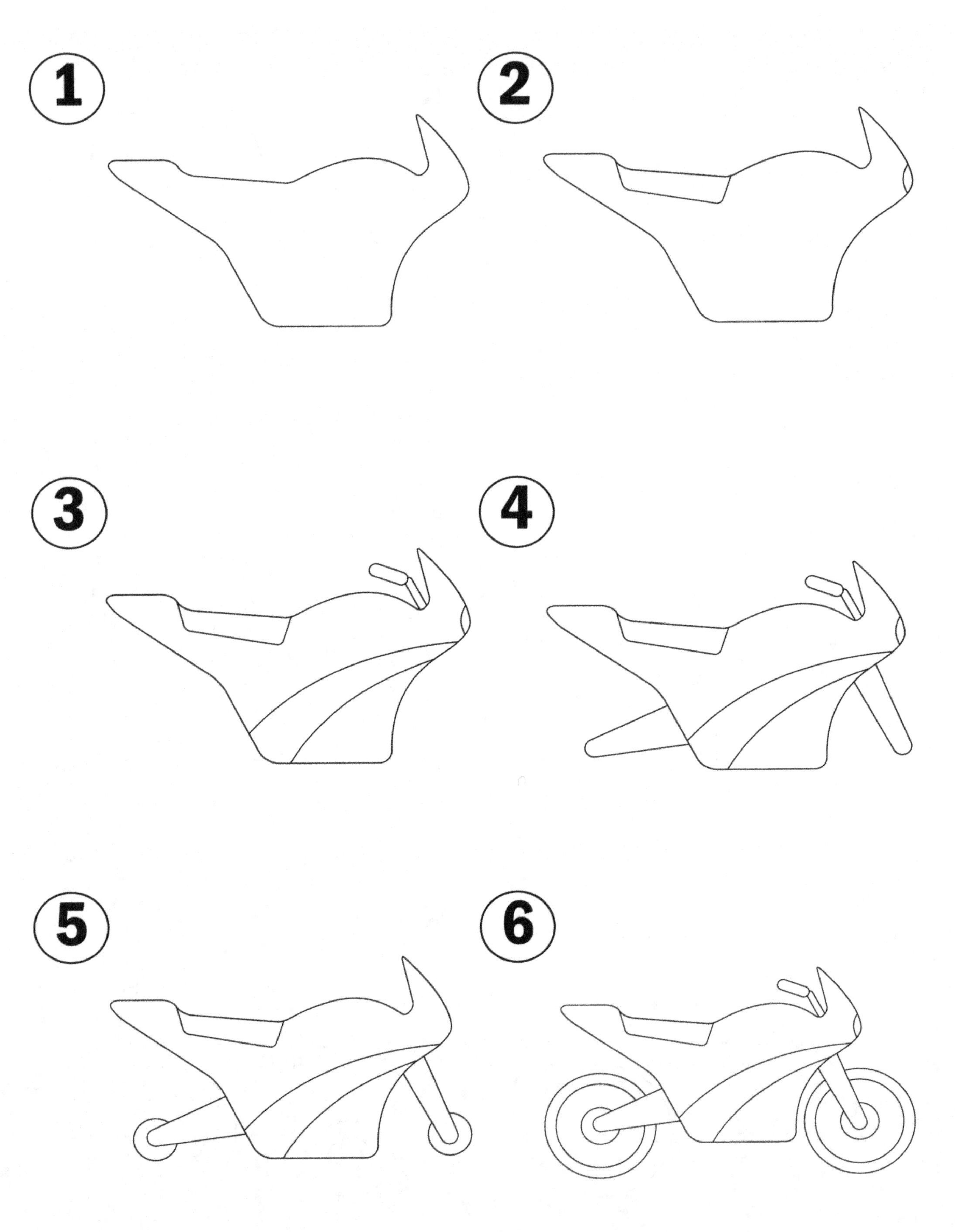

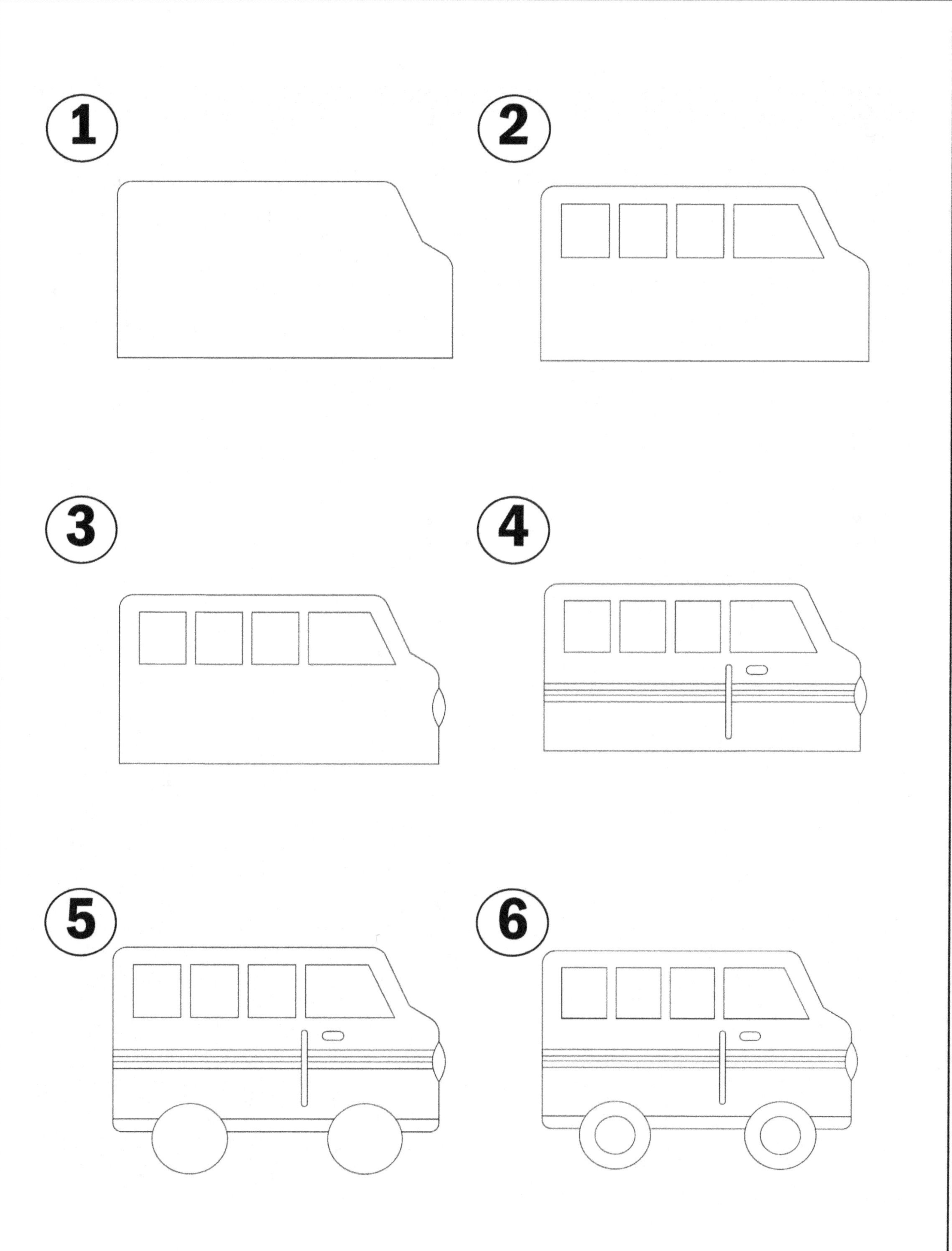

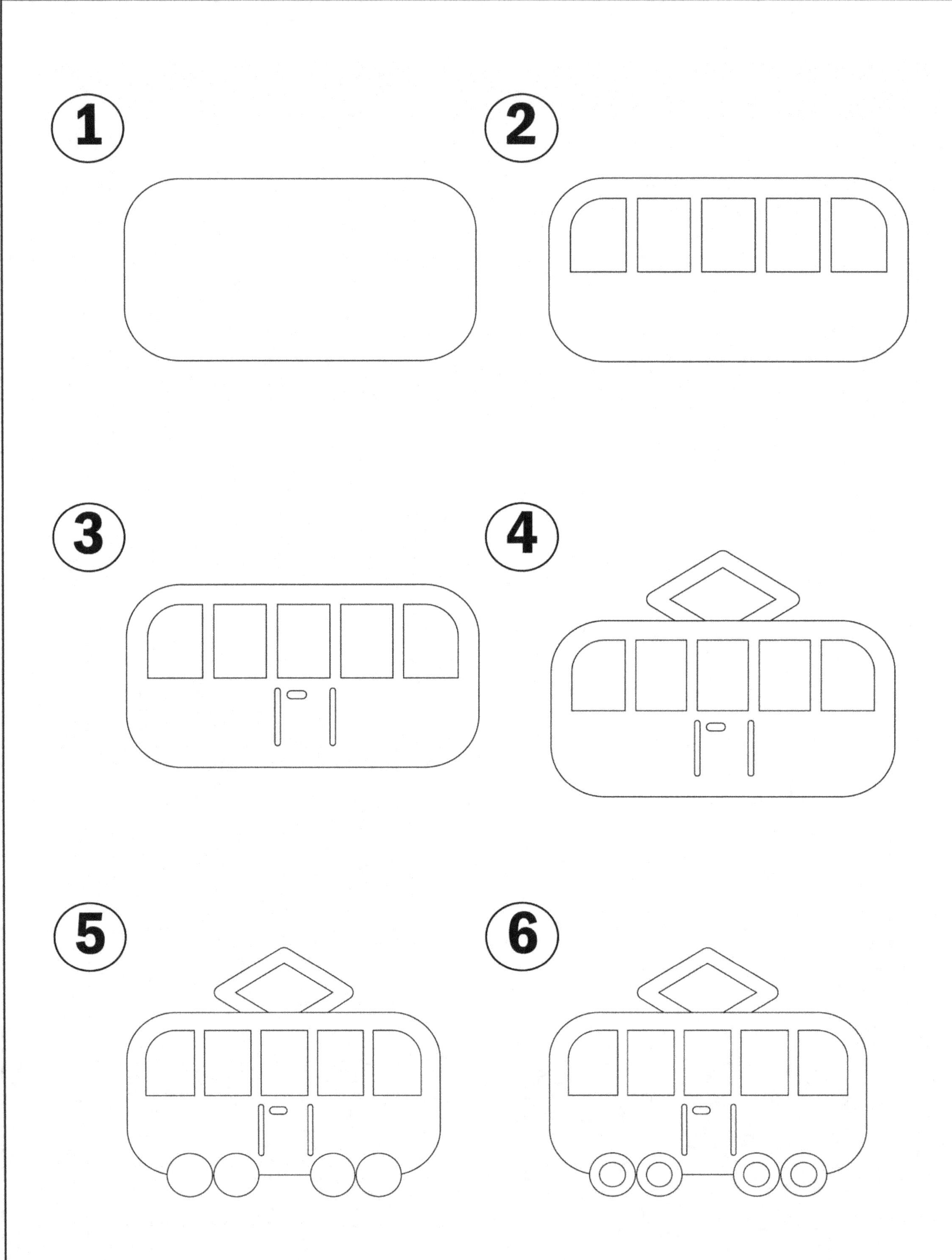

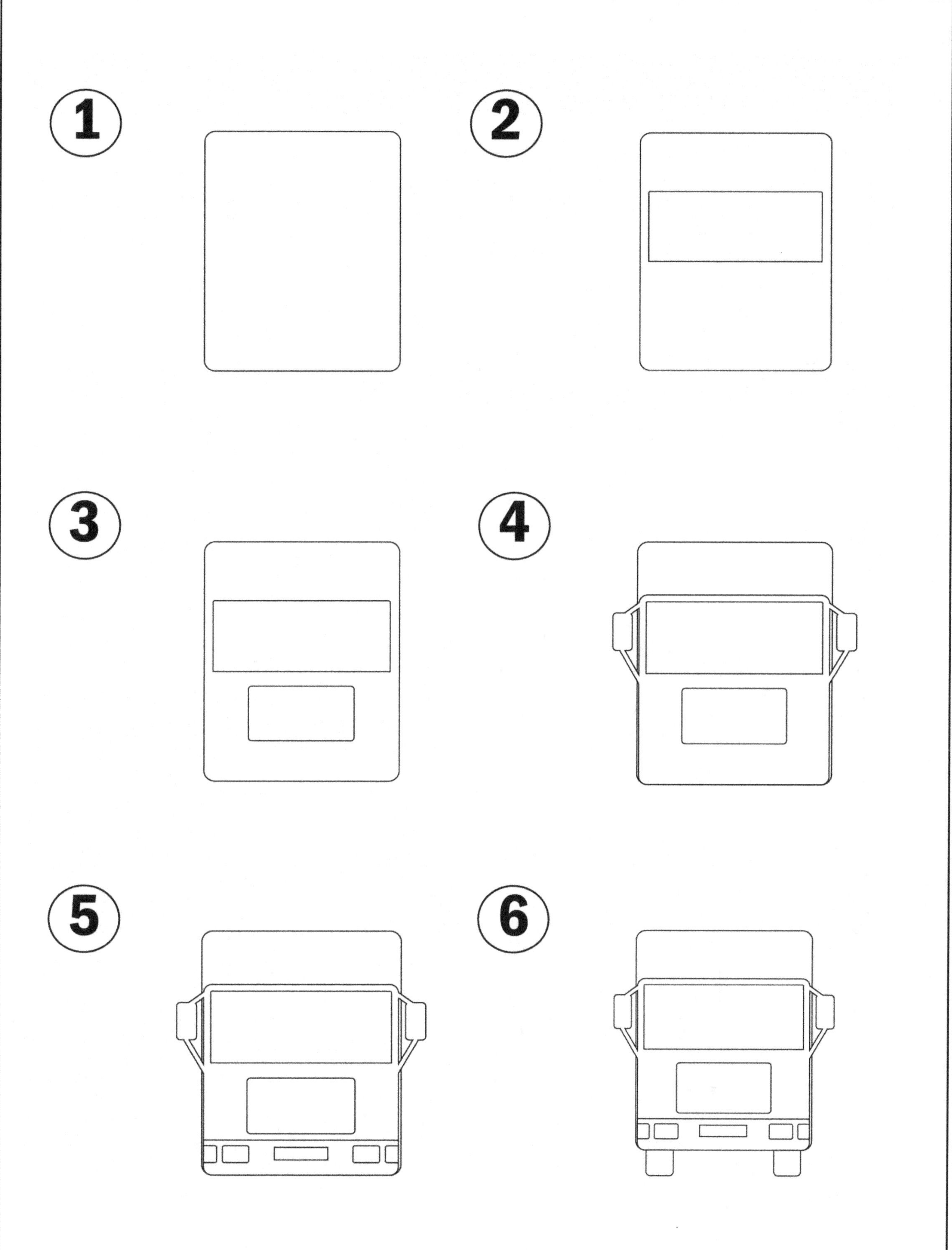

1
2
3
4
5
6

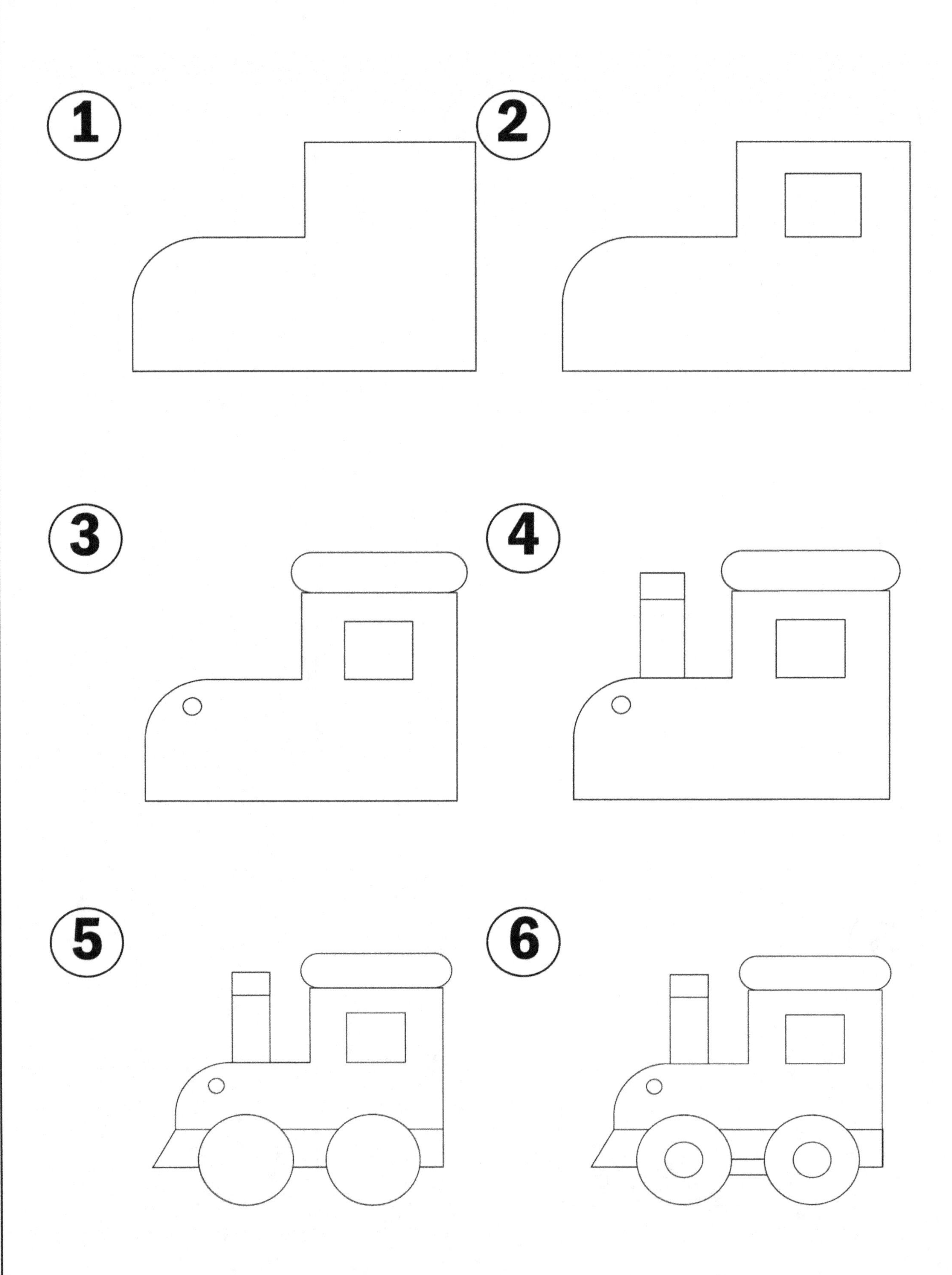

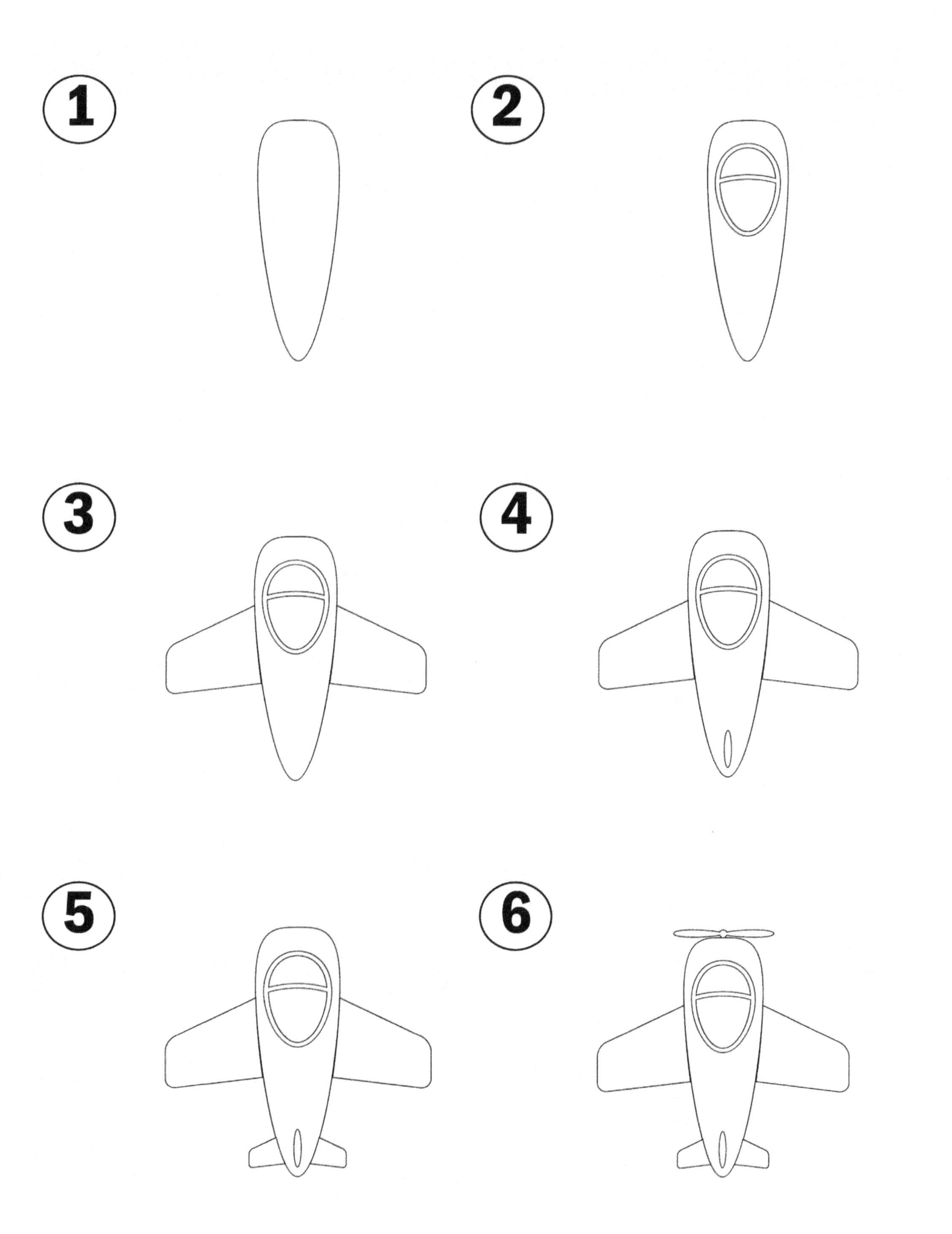

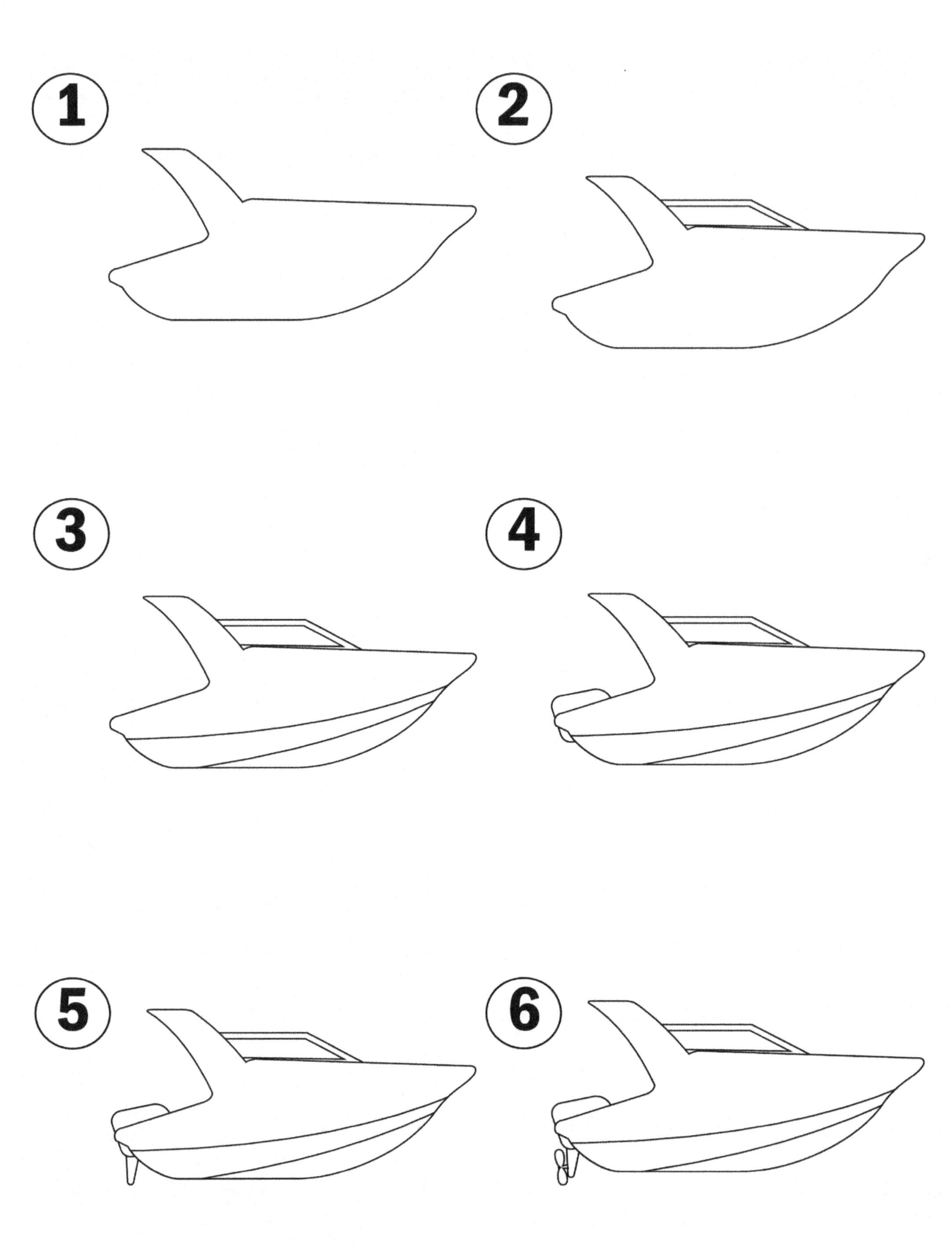

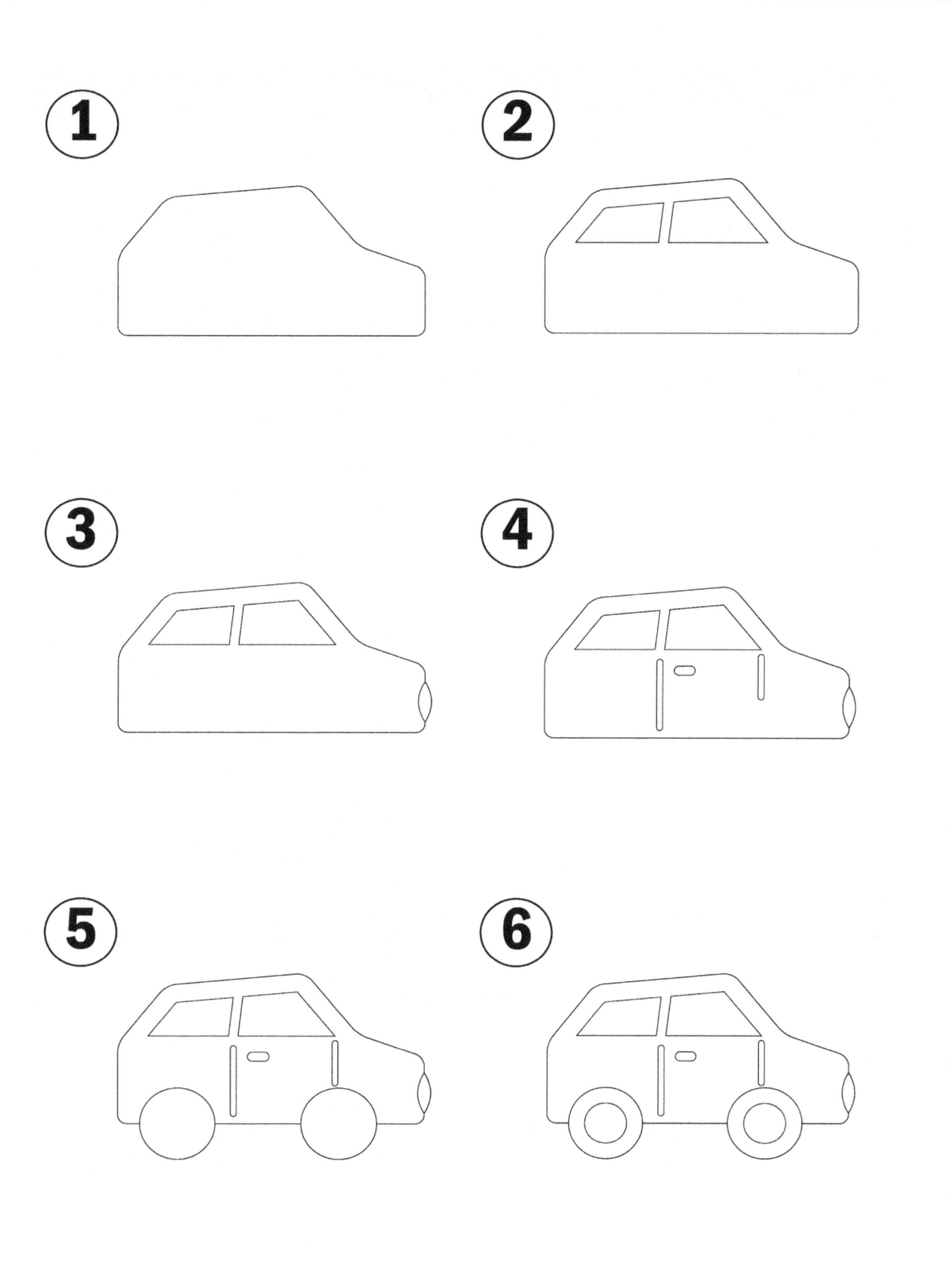

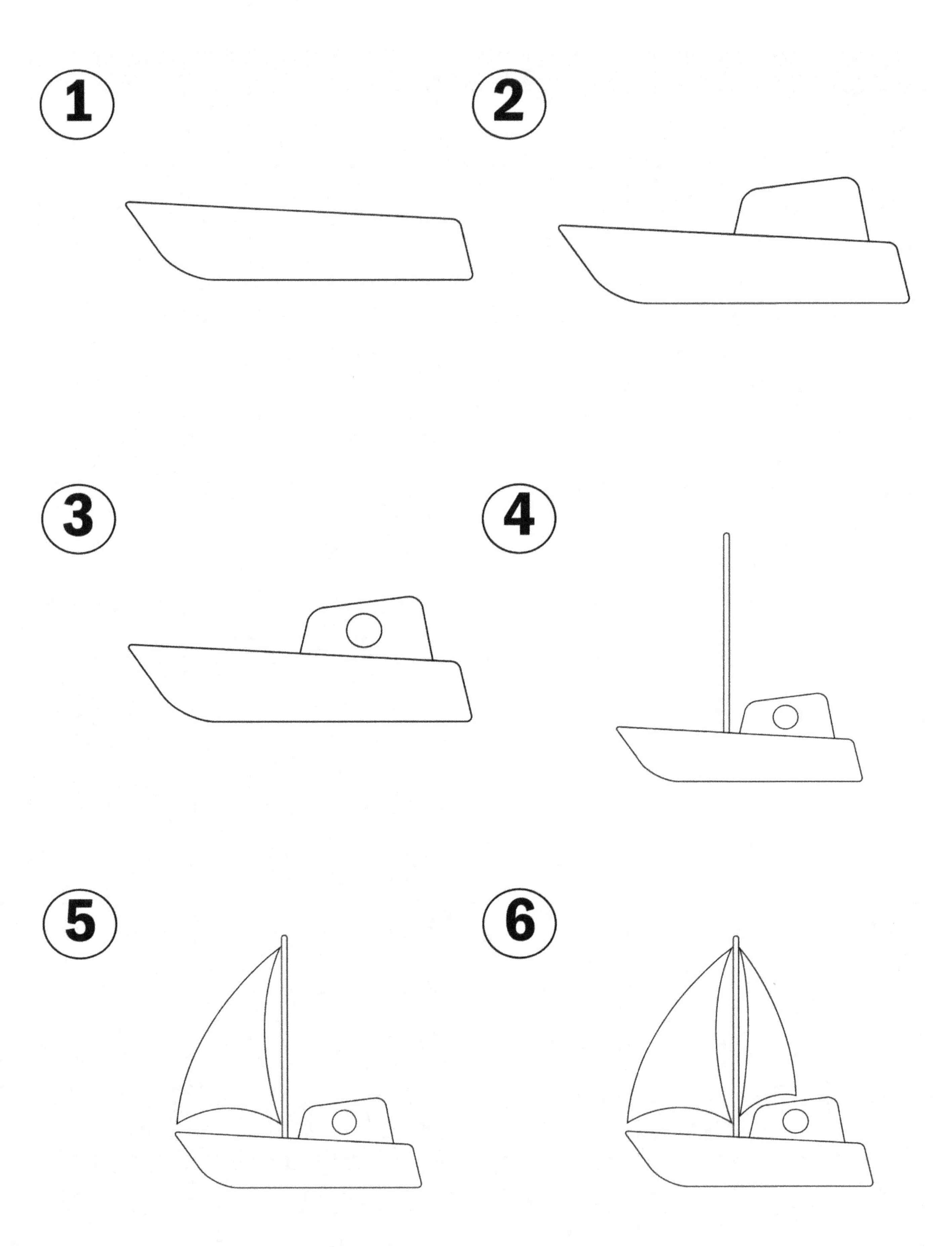
1
2
3
4
5
6

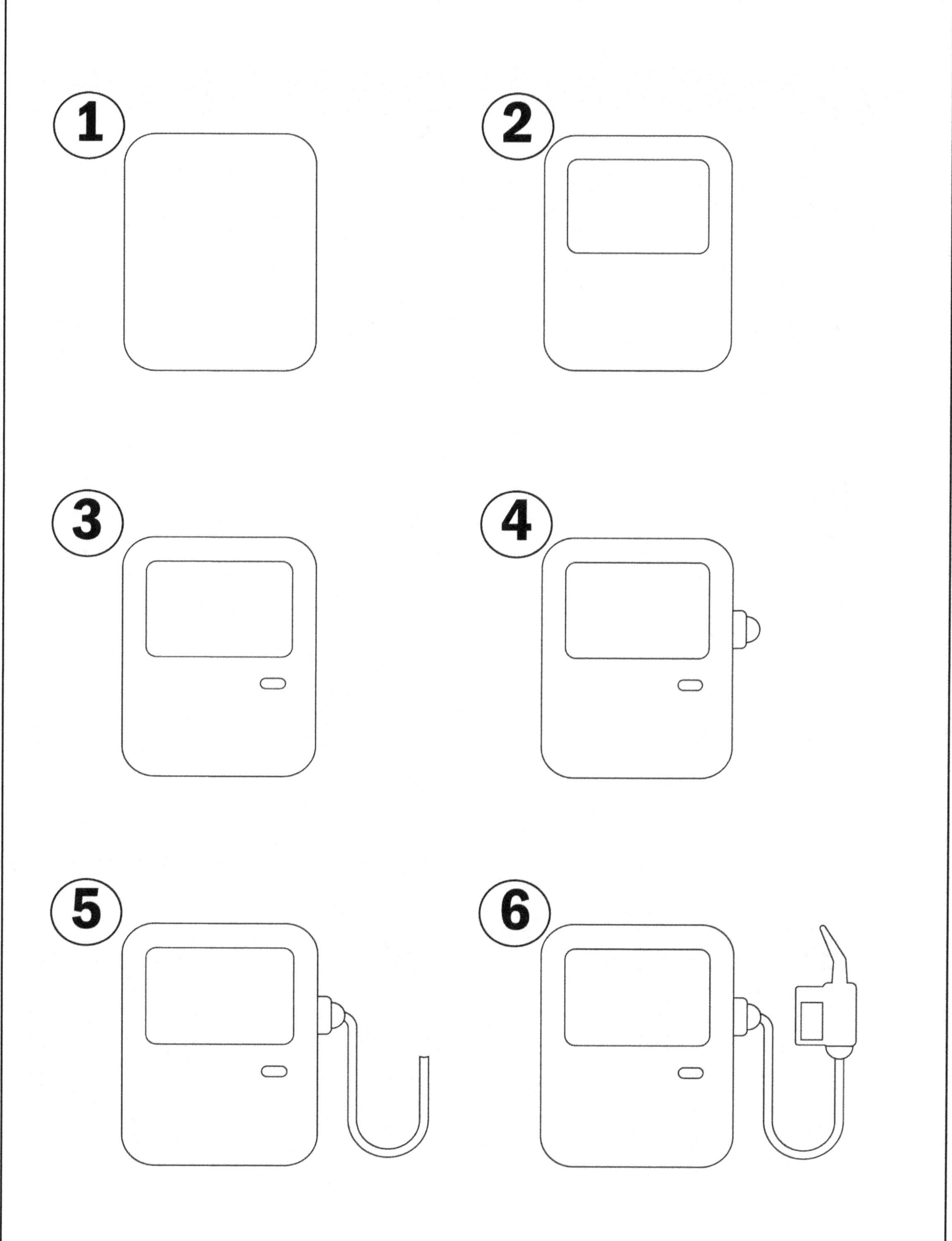

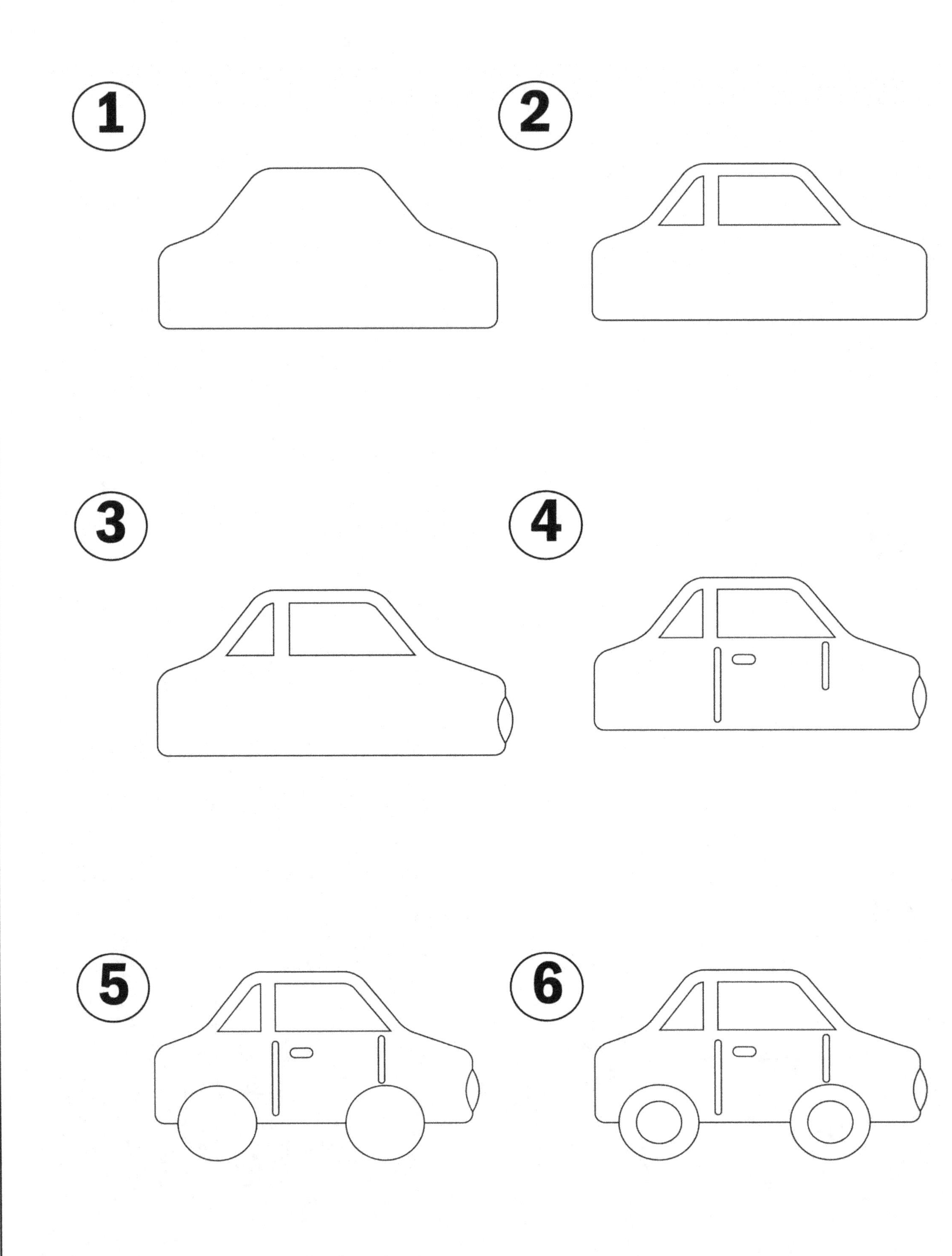

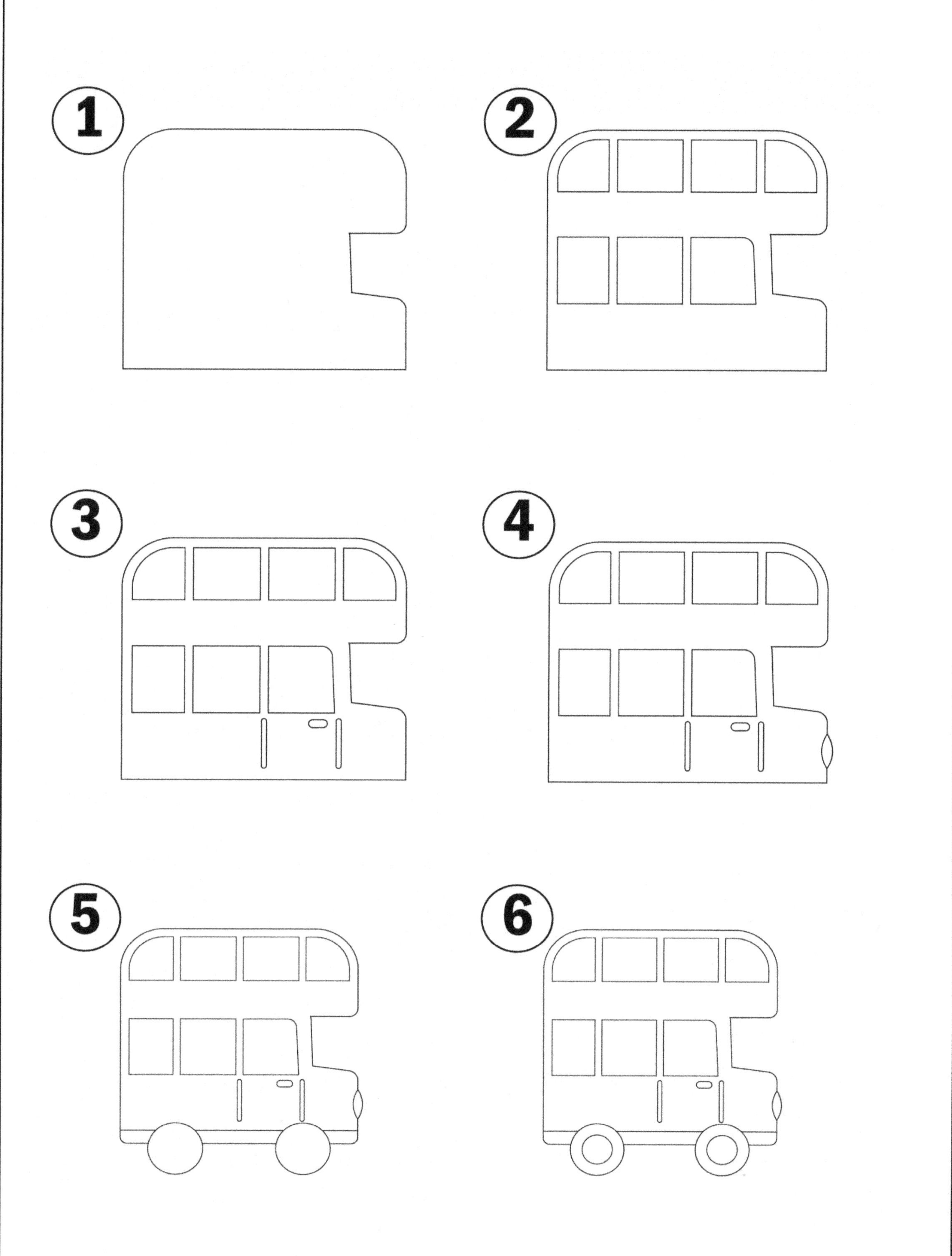

1
2
3
4
5
6

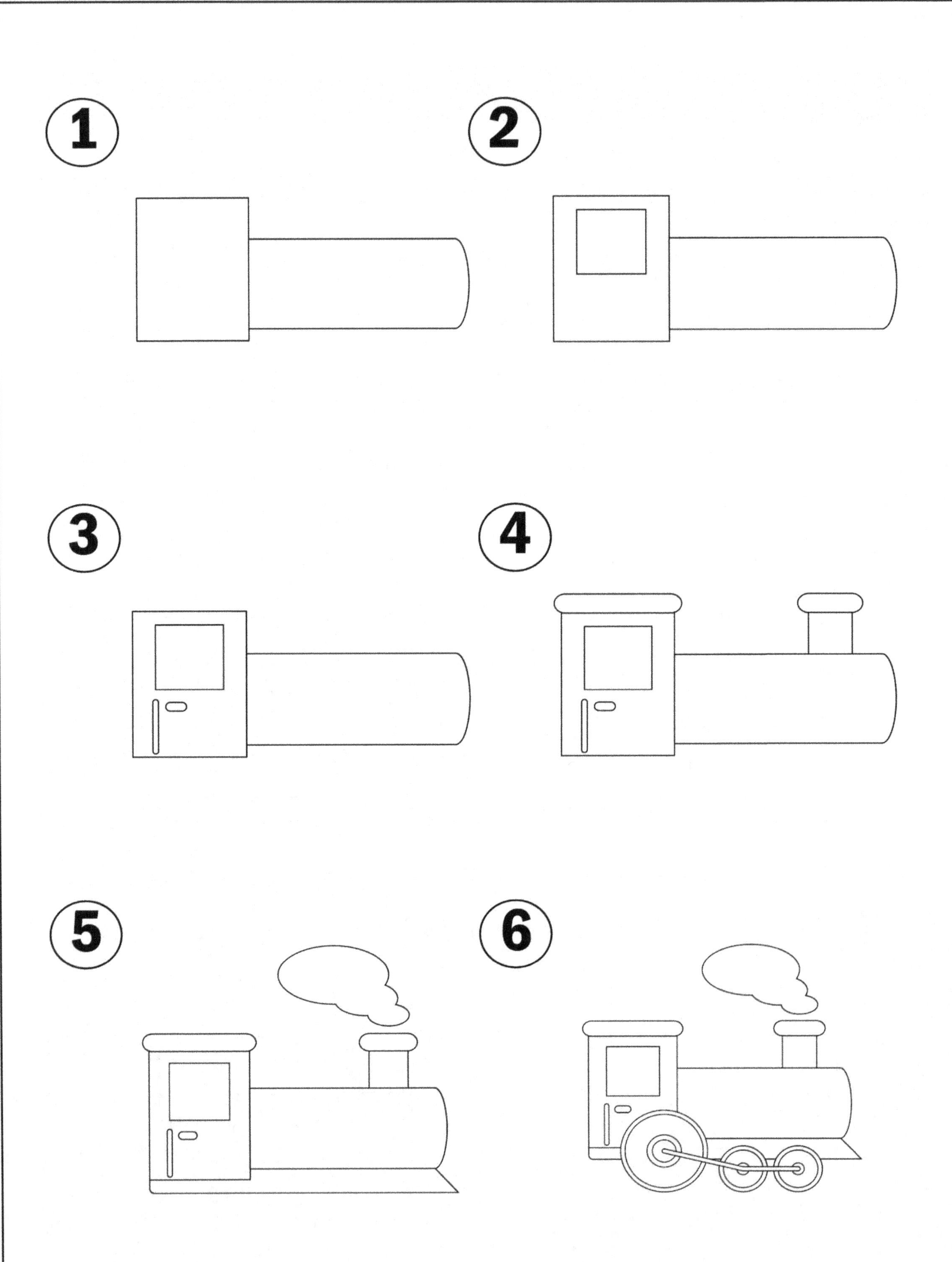

1
2
3
4
5
6

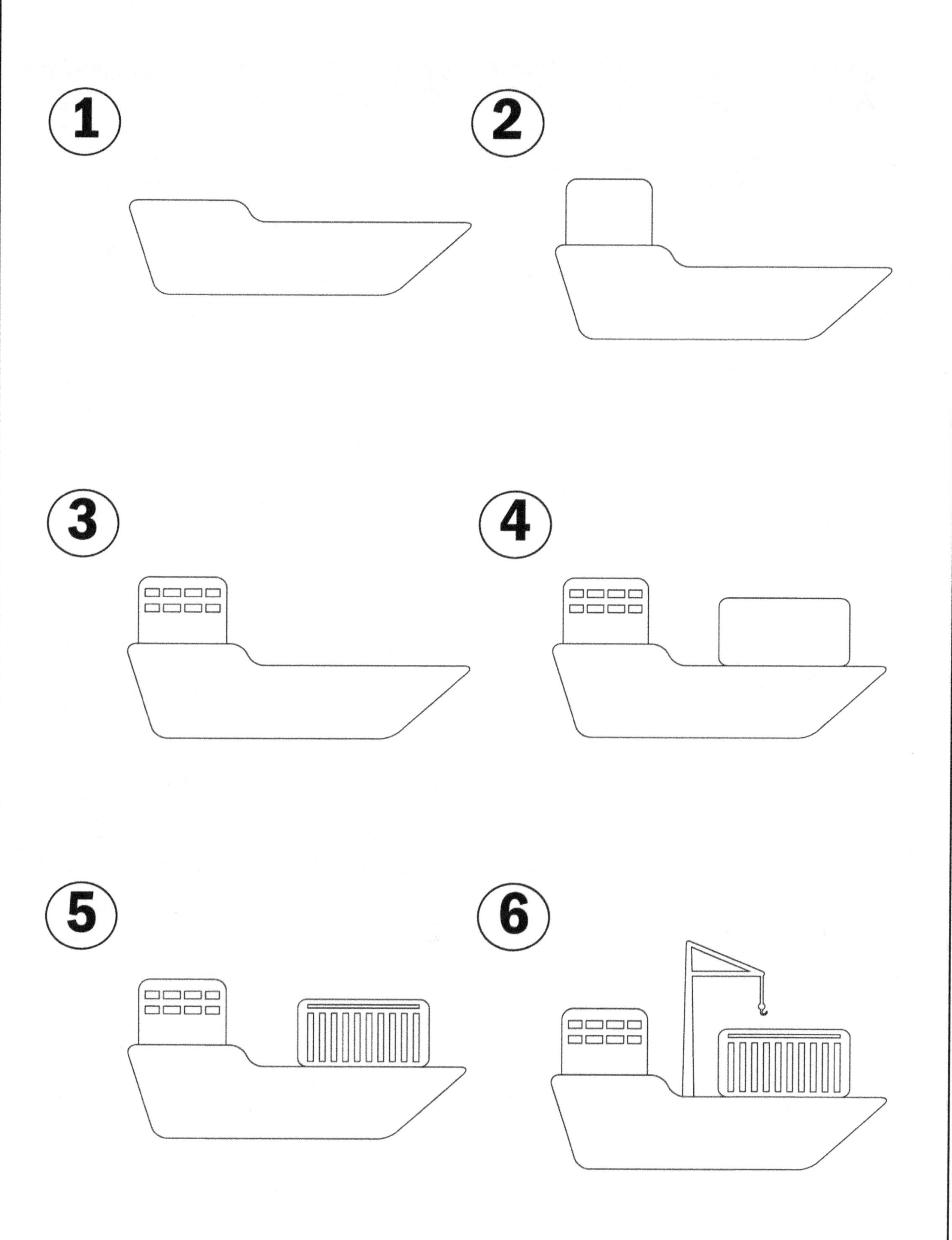

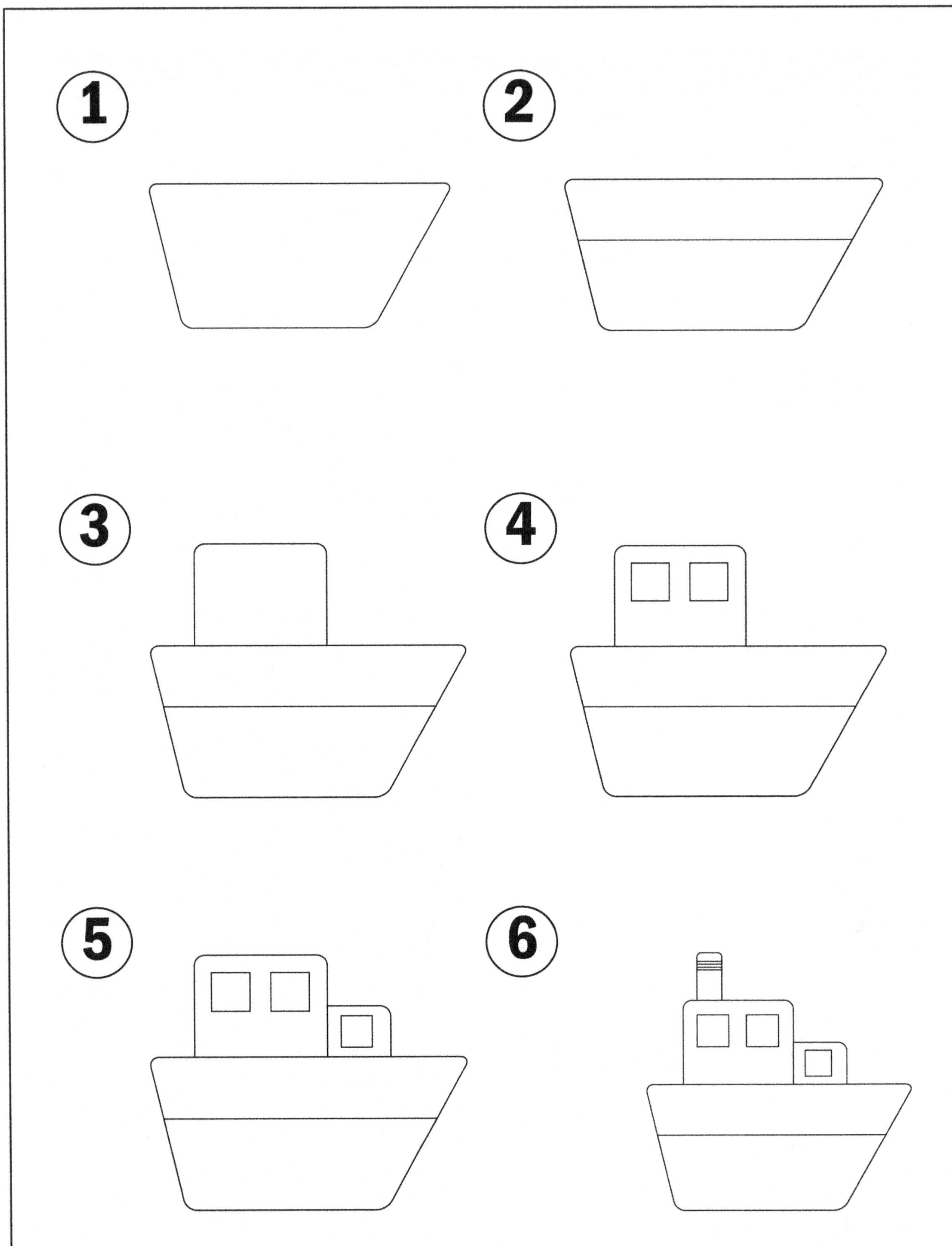

1
2
3
4
5
6

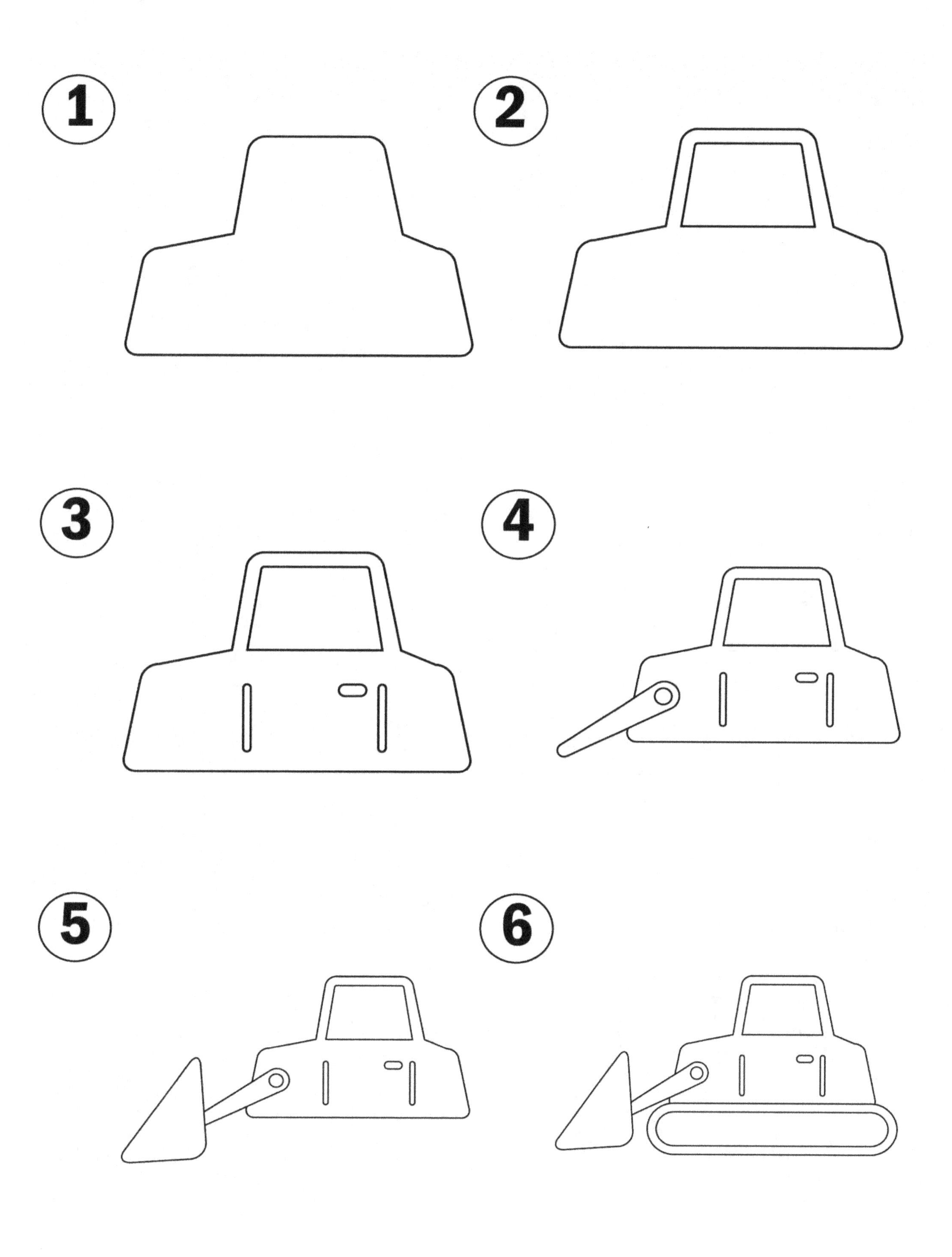

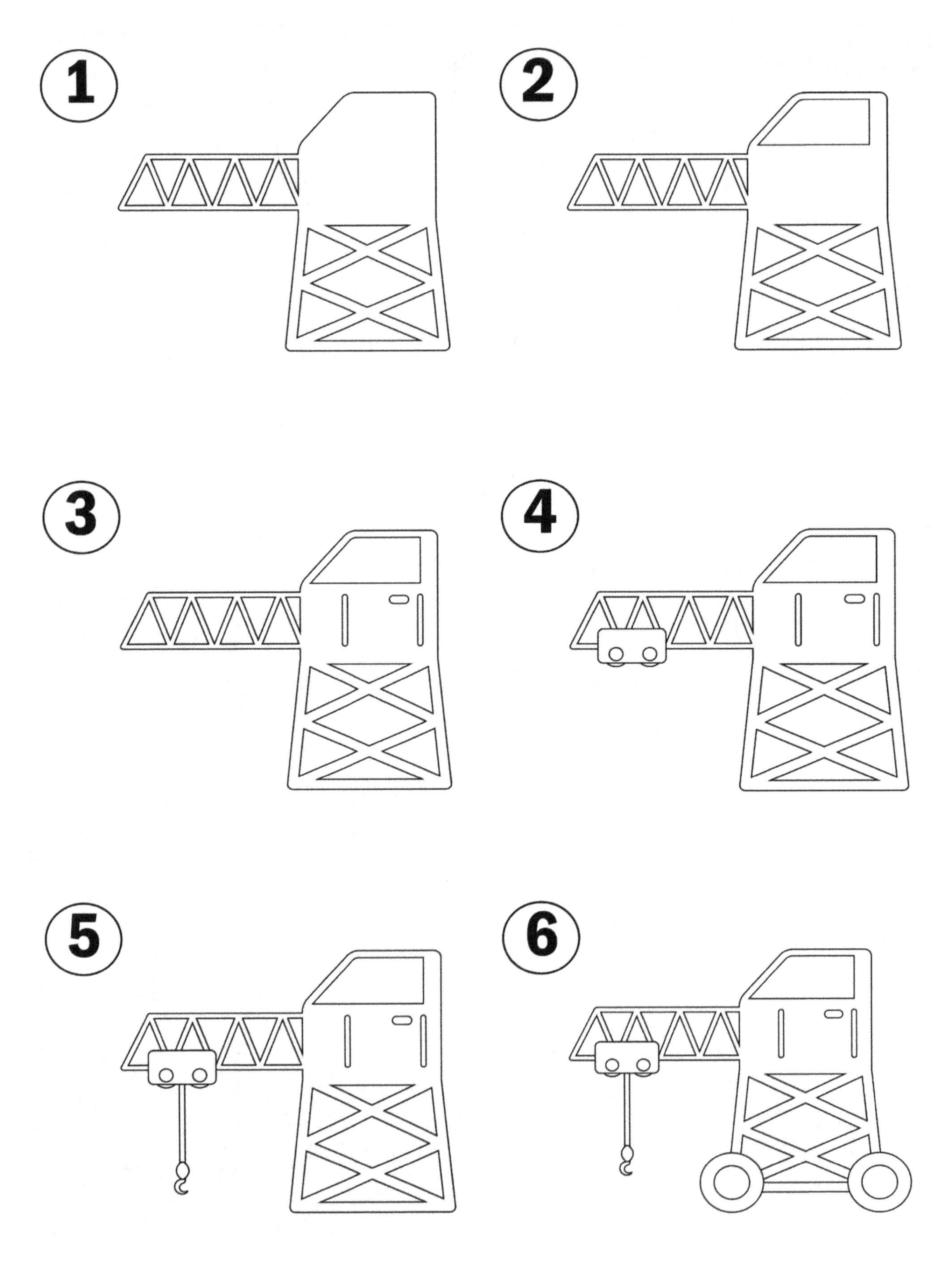

1
2
3
4
5
6

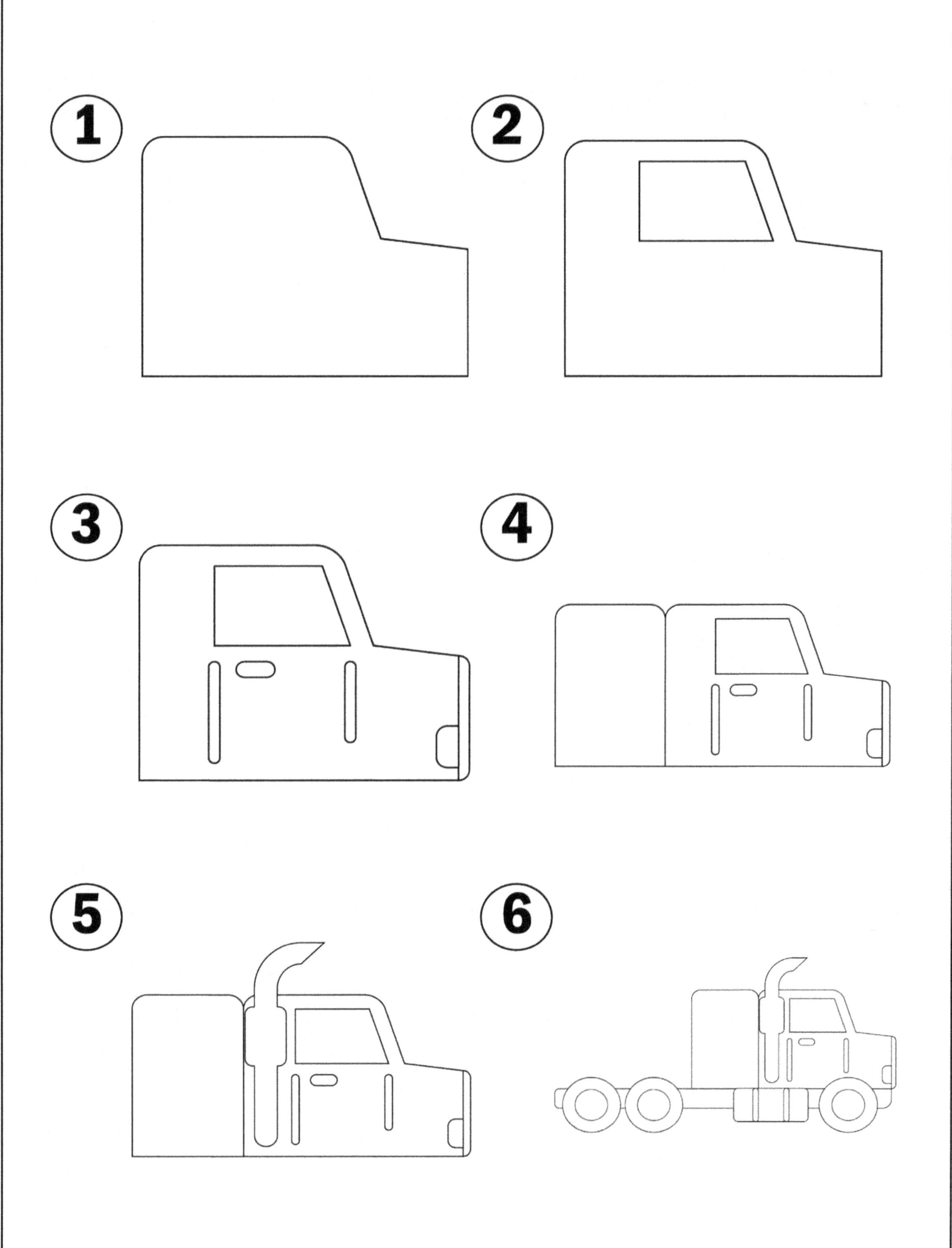

1
2
3
4
5
6

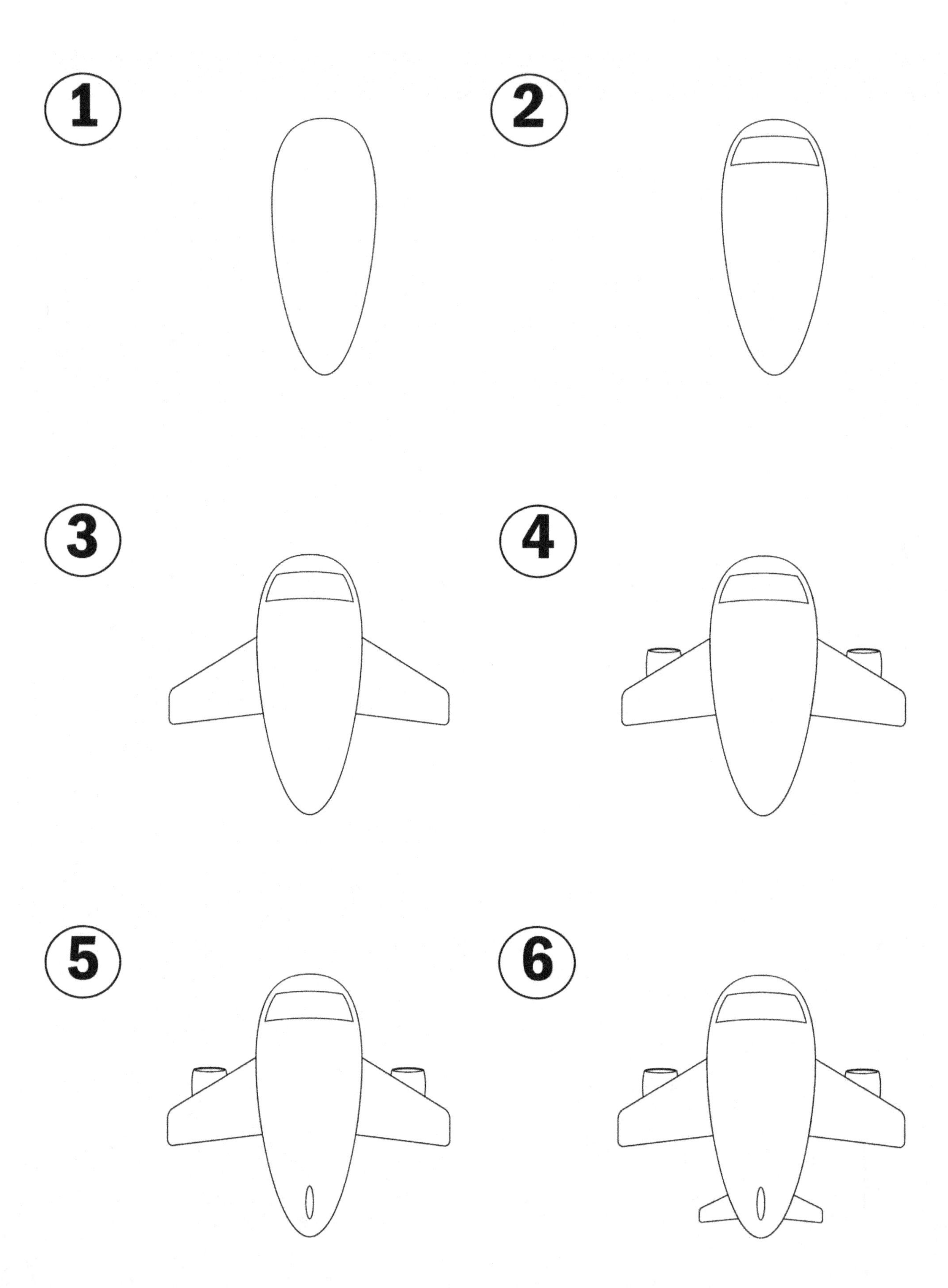

1
2
3
4
5
6

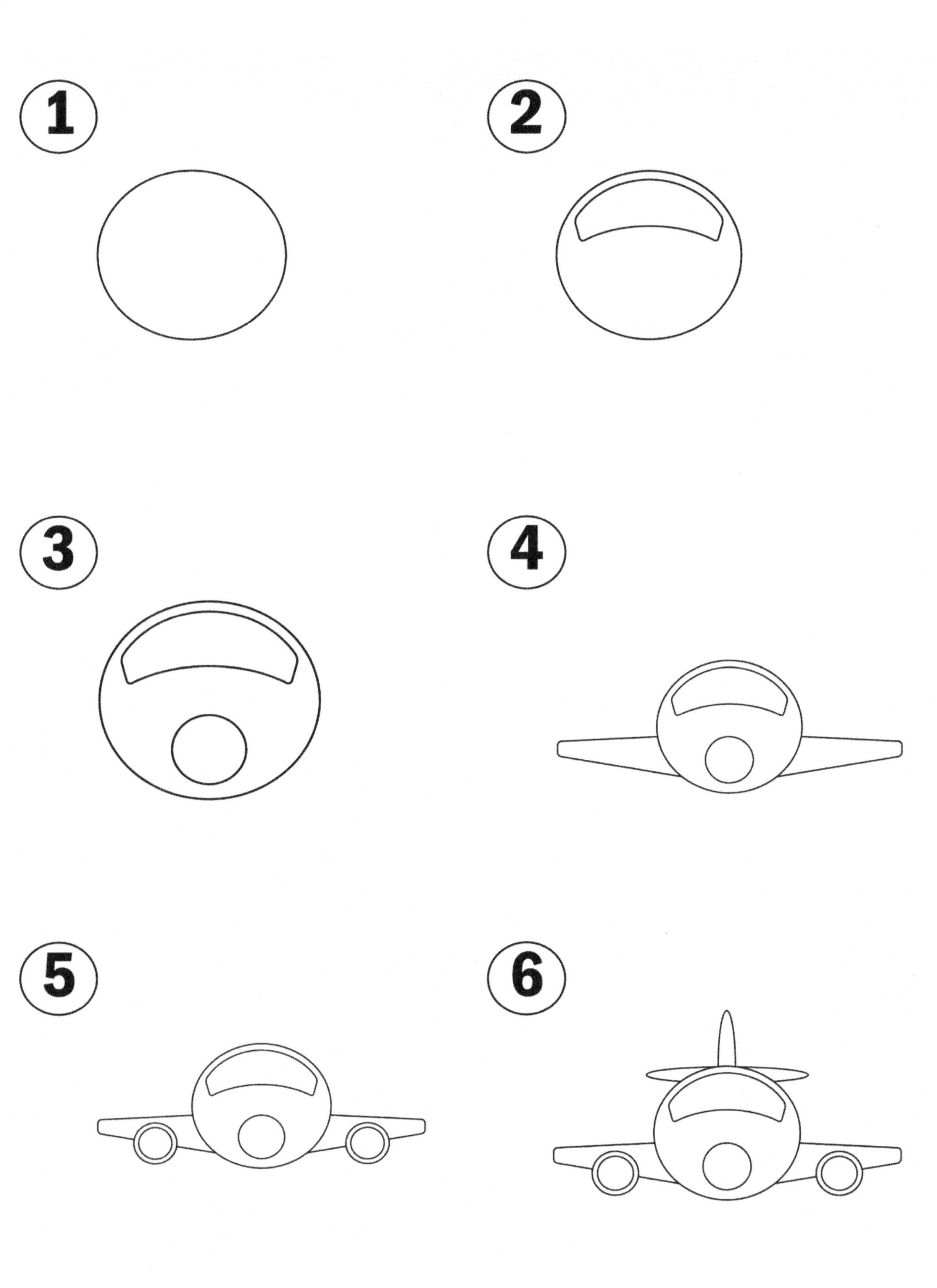

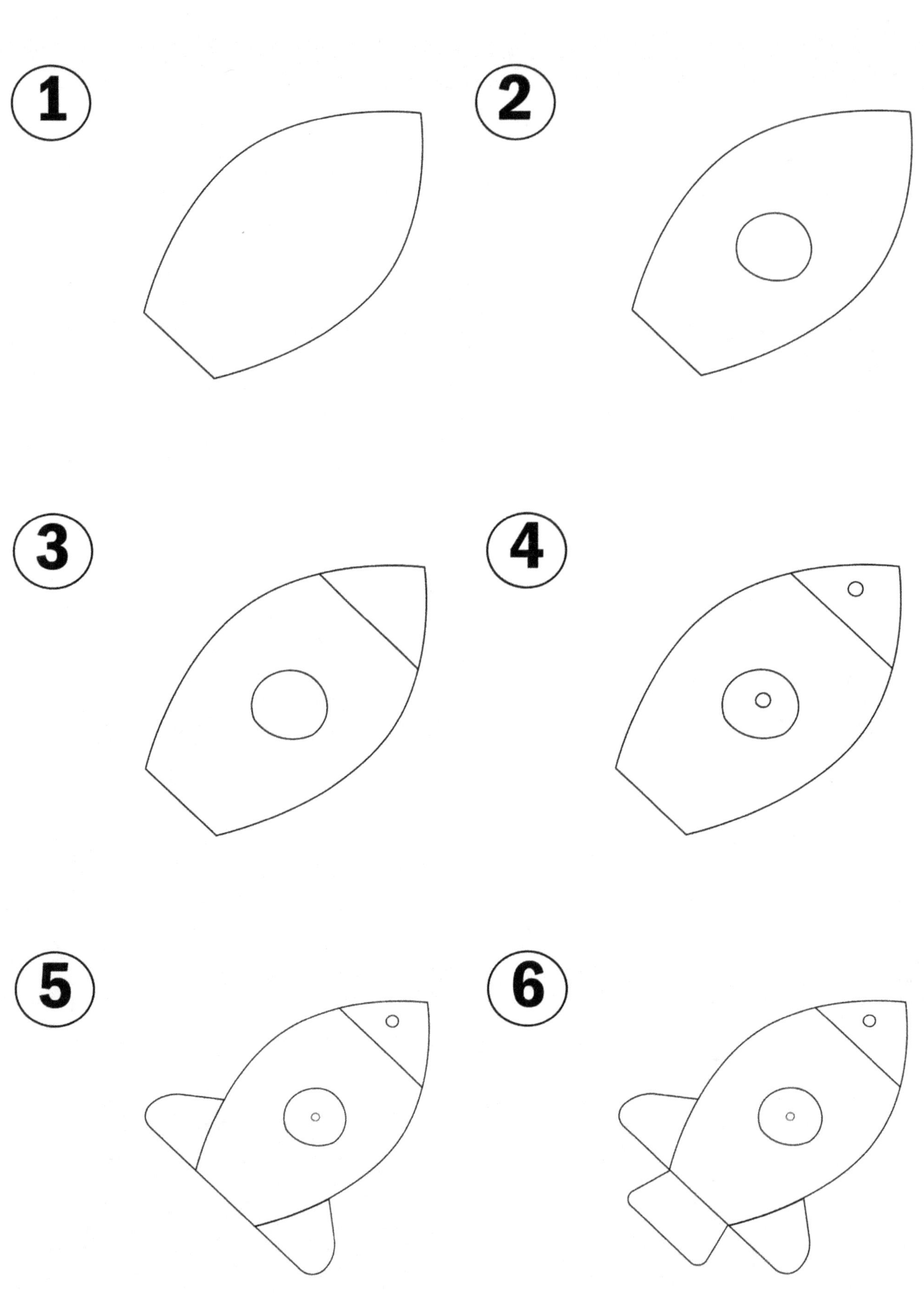